Of Ox and Unicorn

An Immigrant's Story

Of Ox
and Unicorn

An Immigrant's Story

Alan K. Joe

Of Ox and Unicorn

Published by AuthorSource
San Diego, CA
www.authorsourcemedia.com

ISBN: 978-1-947939-10-3
Printed in Canada

Cover design by Christian Kirk-Jensen

To Mother, my best teacher who never went to school.
To Father, who said, "Study hard. No working in laundry."
To my wife, who gives me love, time, and space to write.
To my children and grandchildren,
who give me smiles and meaning to it all.

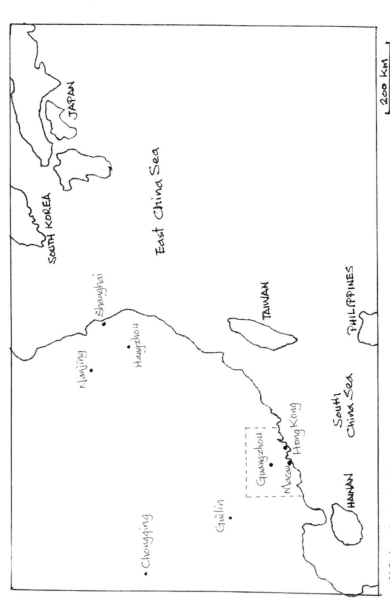

MAP 1 : SOUTH EAST CHINA

200 Km

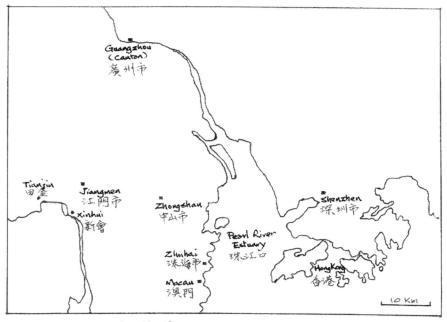

MAP 2 : SOUTHERN GUANGDONG

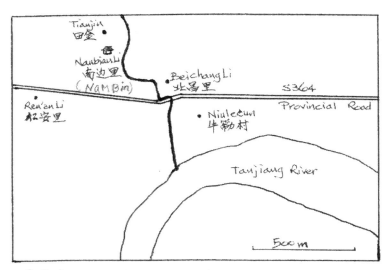

MAP 3 : MY ANCESTRAL VILLAGE

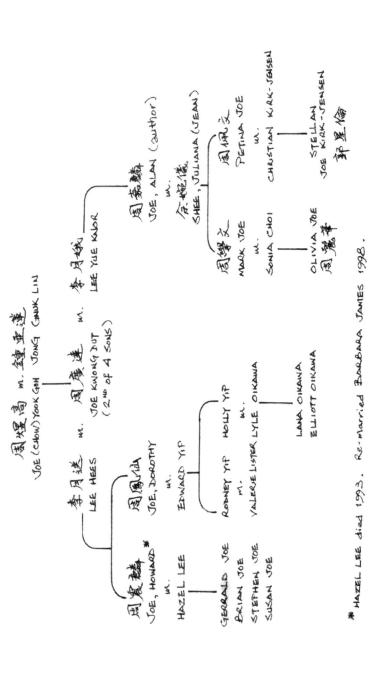

Author's Family Tree beginning with Grandfather Chow (Joe) Yook Goh

TABLE OF CONTENTS

ACKNOWLEDGEMENTS

"Learn to write. Our stories must be told!" My mother told me this when she bought me a diary booklet for my eleventh birthday. Since then, more than thirty volumes of varying sizes have gathered in my drawers, and I relied on them for help. I thank my mother for her foresight.

The writing of this book began ten years ago, and many individuals have helped me. I am forever grateful for their kindness, encouragement, and critique.

My formal training in memoir writing began with Gayle Dzis. A decade ago in her class in Toronto, Canada, she taught me how to write and organize my stories into the first draft of a manuscript. She constantly encouraged me to write and to publish.

Linda Turchen read and critiqued my stories. She offered many excellent suggestions.

While spending the past nine winters in sunny Florida, I enrolled in The Point Brittany Writer's Workshop in St. Petersburg. I learned so much about memoir and creative writing, first from Margaret Emelson, then from Carol Huff, and, for the past five years, from Dr. Muriel Gold, a recipient of the Order of Canada. She did the most to improve my writing and reading. She edited the second draft of my manuscript and wrote the foreword and endorsement for this book. My heartfelt appreciation.

Many friends gave me their time in reading and commenting on my stories, which helped me enormously in making this book readable. I thank them from the depth of my heart:

Dr. Philip Warren, the former Minister of Education for the Province of Newfoundland, who edited my stories, improved my English and boosted my confidence.

Arlene Chan, for her knowledge of the Chinese Communities, her helpful critique and endorsement of this book.

Irene Chu, for her advice, encouragement and help in finding my chief editor.

Reva Stern, for her general evaluation of my manuscript and good recommendations. Christian Kirk-Jensen, for the design of my book cover, and much other help.

Sharon Kettlewell, for teaching me computer skills and word processing. She helped me with the typing, editing, and in more ways than I can count.

Patricia Kennedy, my chief editor, who patiently and skilfully edited, organized, and shaped my stories into a book. My heartfelt thanks for all of her assistance.

Thanks to our nephew Andrew Shee for the maps and family tree; our daughter-in-law Sonia for her computer expertise and help.

Contributing significantly to my "Art of Writing" were all my friends from my writing classes in Toronto and St. Petersburg.

Julia Avis and Cecilia Chan, for editing some of my stories.

Many thanks to Beth Lottig and Simon Presland for their expertise and help in the publication of this book.

Lastly, I wish to acknowledge the reader, whoever you are, for reading my stories.

Thanks to all of you!

FOREWORD

Alan Joe joined our Point Brittany Writers Workshop in St Petersburg, Florida, several years ago. At that time, I was co-leading the workshop with Carol Huff, an educator and creative writing teacher. When Carol took ill, I assumed the sole leadership of the group and continue to conduct it at present. When I began to lead the workshop solo, my theatre background – artistic director and theatre educator – prompted me to augment the writing sessions with a staged reading of my writers' works. These readings became an annual event, with audiences increasing considerably each year.

When I first broached this idea to the group, Alan Joe approached me quietly to ask a favour. Would I give him private coaching on his written piece, "Ginger Tea for Mother?" I readily agreed. However, my direction took him by surprise. "My goodness, you are coaching me for a performance, not a reading, I am an orthodontist, not an actor, he exclaimed."

"Yes, but you can be an actor, Alan," I countered. And I was right. He had a natural ability to respond to direction, with the result that each year his presentations are especially anticipated by the spectators. Of course, the dramatic content of his material obviously plays a significant role in his moving deliveries. The cliché "not a dry eye in the house" applies in his case.

From the beginning, it was clear that Alan Joe had a fascinating story to tell, both from a personal as well as a historical perspective. The reader of this book will discover that he is a meticulous writer, and has an uncanny talent for describing the smallest details of his bittersweet experiences. His "To Kill a Clucking Bird" evokes sweet memories of his introduction to Toronto, while "An Enemy in My Bed" depicts a horrifying event he suffered as a small boy in China. His poetic eulogy to his mother is written with both love and humility. Dr. Alan Joe is thoughtful, intelligent, and a history buff. In discussions with him, I often feel that he missed his vocation. He has a profound knowledge of historical events and a love of history in general.

Of Ox and Unicorn is a contribution not only to the Canadian Chinese community, but also to immigrants in other countries and of different faiths, and to the general reader.

It is with great pleasure that I introduce you to this excellent autobiography.

Muriel Gold, CM, PhD
Author of *Tell Me Why Nights Are Lonesome* (a family history)
and six additional books

WAR, PEACE,
AND A NEW LIFE

1

BORN TO FLEE

From the moment I was born, I was on the run. My mother told me this story many times: "You were born to flee. We ran and hid when you were only a few hours old. On the glorious morning of July 21, 1937, when I was happily nursing you, suddenly sirens screamed. A panicky nurse rushed into our maternity ward and shouted, 'Air raid! Air raid! It's the Japs. Everyone to the shelter. Quick! Quick! Follow me. Hurry!'"

Two weeks before my birth, Japanese soldiers had attacked the Chinese garrison at the Marco Polo Bridge near Beijing (Peking). This gun battle ignited Japan's horrific eight-year invasion of China, which would last until 1945. I was born in the Year of the Ox, according to the Chinese zodiac. On that fateful morning, Mother quickly pulled me off her breast and ran after the nurse and the other mothers. They scampered down two flights of stairs to the basement of the Dong Wah Hospital in the city of Guangzhou (Canton), Guangdong, China. In the makeshift bomb shelter, she was packed into a room that smelled of formaldehyde and disinfectant, a morgue.

Squeezed into a dank corner, she sat with her knees drawn up, careful not to push her feet against the plastered leg of a man standing on crutches. To keep me quiet, my mother stuffed her nipple back into my mouth, and cooled me with her paper folding fan. She was trembling, terrified of losing me, because she had already lost a two-year-old son, four years earlier. Fervently she prayed, "Buddha, have mercy. Quan Yin, have mercy!"

Fortunately, on that day no bombs fell on our city, and after an hour of cowering in the sweltering heat, everyone filed out of the shelter.

A month later, as a Chinese custom, my parents gave a party to celebrate my one full month birthday, in which I was given my name. For the Chinese, naming a child appropriately is a matter of great significance. An infant's name reflects the hope that the child will attain the qualities the name implies, and the belief is that it will later determine a person's character and destiny.

My father announced to the assembled guests that I was to be called Kar Lun in Cantonese, which I interpreted it to mean "Honourable Unicorn." Legend tells that the Chinese unicorn, called Ki Lun in Cantonese or Qilin in Mandarin, is a spiritual and blessed creature. According to Wikipedia, the Chinese unicorn has features of various animals. Its head might look like that of a dragon. It can have the body of a deer, the tail of an ox, and a horn on its forehead. It is often compared to the unicorn of Western mythology, which is usually depicted as a white horse with a long horn. On the night our sage Confucius was born, the story goes that a Ki Lun visited his mother, bearing in his mouth a jade tablet, engraved with a poem in praise of her soon-to-be-born son. As I was born in the year of the Ox, my father thought that the noble unicorn should balance well with the lowly, labouring ox. The Ox person is described as being hard-working, conscientious, and loyal – and may at times appear dumb, much like me.

As our guests were savouring a traditional appetizer of roasted suckling pig and young sweet ginger, sirens screamed. From our apartment balcony, my mother said that she could see three bird-like dots in the distance, swooping down fast. Many guests left quickly, while my father led the others to the ground-floor apartment of a Mr. and Mrs. Wang, thinking it would be safest there, since our building did not have a basement, and there weren't any air-raid shelters nearby.

In the apartment of the Wangs, my parents huddled with a few others under the big dining table, made of solid ebony. My mother held me tight to her bosom as bombers roared overhead. Boom! Boom! Boom! The earth shook and windows shattered, sending debris flying every which way. Some jagged pieces of glass hit my mother; the others were only slightly hurt. Luckily, my father found a rickshaw on a main street near our house, and Mother was rushed to the hospital. After my parents waited for hours in an overcrowded and cacophonous emergency room, full of victims of the bombing, a doctor finally took a quick look at her wounds, left a nurse with some instructions, and hurried away. The nurse gave my mother an injection and dug out the shards; then she too rushed off. My mother said I slept fitfully in her arms and cried a lot, startled by the constant moaning and crying of the wounded and dying.

Several buildings in a nearby commercial street suffered direct hits, and many were killed or injured. Fire and smoke blackened the sky, and ambulances and fire engines continued to scream throughout the day, well into the dark night of terror.

We were on the run to avoid the bombing. In a matter of three months, we fled from Canton to my eldest aunt's home in Kong Moon, to Grandma Lee's in a village called Leen Tong, and briefly to our ancestral house in Nam Bin, all within approximately a hundred miles further inland from Hong Kong. Finally, my father settled my mother and me in Hong Kong. He thought that this colony was secure, because it was guarded by the mighty British Empire. Nevertheless, Mother felt uneasy, because she heard rumours that the British regarded this colony as an outpost, and its garrison was relatively small, likely no match against the superior forces of the Japanese.

Shanghai was the financial centre of China; it fell to the Japanese in November 1937. China's capital at the time, Nanking (now Nanjing), located some 190 miles up the Yangtze River from Shanghai, was the next target for the Japanese onslaught. Her navy began to blockade the coast of China, choking off her shipping with the outside world.

My father had another family in Canada, a wife and two children in Toronto. Traditionally many Chinese men married multiple wives if they could afford it, and nearly all marriages were arranged by matchmakers. He decided that he must leave my mother, who was his second wife, with me in Hong Kong. He had to return to North America before the Japanese navy blockaded the entire coast of China, making it too dangerous to cross the Pacific Ocean. In November 1937, he sailed for Vancouver, Canada.

Meanwhile, Japanese forces continued their aggression and occupied much more Chinese territory, including my hometown of Guangzhou, about a hundred miles from Hong Kong. Wherever they went, they raped, looted, and killed, spreading terror throughout the country.

Growing up, my mother reminded me time and again: "You were born to flee, a helpless fugitive. We suffered. We survived. Cherish your life and do some good with it!"

2

A STRANGE ENCOUNTER IN KOWLOON

I had a strange encounter in Kowloon, a district located on the mainland, opposite to Victoria Island, which the Chinese called Hong Kong. For the first three and a half years of my life, after my father returned to Canada, I lived there with my mother. I was curious about the many strange-looking white people on the streets, particularly men dressed in uniforms, some in greenish skirts and colourful long socks. The ladies wore all manner of dress, and their hair was not black like mine and my mother's. I saw dark brown, red, blonde, or something in between. My mother told me these people were called Quilo, "pale ghosts," meaning foreigners. My older cousin Ho Gor explained further that most of these foreigners had come from Britain, which had grabbed Hong Kong as a colony, by beating up the Chinese in the Opium War. Not until I was much older did I understand this story fully, but at the time I disliked Quilo and was actually afraid of them.

One October evening, my mother and I were out walking and shopping. I was dazzled by the flashing neon signs and the different sights, smells, and sounds of this strange metropolis, so different from my hometown. People were everywhere: eating at sidewalk stands, spitting out husks of melon seeds, and bargaining loudly with peddlers. Vendors and hawkers were calling out for folks to come and taste their won ton noodles, chicken-rice congee, or chestnuts roasting in sweet molasses. My mother held my hand tightly, because of the noisy crowd and the busy traffic. A sinewy puller, with a white man riding in his rickshaw, was running barefooted, weaving in and out of traffic. He brushed past me, nearly knocking me down.

We entered a Bata store, and Mother bought me a pair of leather shoes. The proprietor told us a new barbecue shop had opened just that morning across the road, and that we should try its tasty roasted pig with crunchy, brown skin. I looked outside and could see fragments of red paper scattered all over the pavement, from spent firecrackers celebrating the grand opening of the restaurant. A pig and several golden geese or ducks hung by the window. My mouth watered. Suddenly, I was so very hungry, and I told my mother that I was weak, starving, and dying. She ignored my entreaties, saying that we had to save our money, and that we had leftovers at home to eat. Besides, earlier in the day, I had already had my treat of the week, a small glass of milk with a lump of sugar and a biscuit. She also said, "You have new shoes. Stop moaning!" I refused to listen, and sulked. She wrapped me in a Chinese sling that had a red and gold dragon embroidered on it. She hoisted me up onto her back, and tied the four straps, two over her shoulders and two around her waist.

Slowly she started walking, while I whimpered. Suddenly, a giant face appeared before me. It hovered momentarily over my head. I looked up to see a massive red beard, a big crooked nose, a mop of reddish hair, and jade-green eyes. What a frightening sight! He ruffled my hair, made a monkey face, and smiled. I recoiled, speechless. He laughed, spoke some strange tongue, and dropped something into my lap. Then he waved and walked away. My little hands found the shiniest red fruit I had ever seen – a big apple. Who was this Quilo? And what was this for?

Standing by the door of a nearby jewellery store was a tall, dark man in uniform, carrying a rifle by his side. He saw us looking puzzled and came over to us. I saw a thick beard and mustache, with a headgear of white cloth wrapped around his head. In halting Cantonese, he explained to Mother that Westerners were celebrating the Autumn Festival, something similar to Halloween. That day I didn't get my wish for a slice of the roasted pig or goose. However, I began to like Quilo. For me, this encounter was a positive introduction to Western people.

Soon after this incident, my mother heard grave rumours that the Japanese were preparing to attack Hong Kong, and possibly to go to war with the United States of America. President Franklin Roosevelt was putting an embargo on the export of oil to Japan. (Importing American oil shipped from California to Japan was a critical lifeline for that country's imperial armed forces and industry.)

Without my father present to consult, my mother made the decision to get away, moving first to the small Portuguese colony of Macau, some thirty-eight miles across the water from Hong Kong.

It was lucky that we did. The Japanese soon attacked; the British, East Indian, local Chinese, and Canadian forces defended Hong Kong heroically for eighteen days. With huge loss of life, and without any reinforcements from Britain, Hong Kong surrendered on Christmas Day, 1941.

A year later, we moved again, to our ancestral village of Nam Bin in the county of Xin Hui. My mother thought the enemy would not bother us in a poor rural village, where the cost of living was lower. Unfortunately, the enemy penetrated everywhere. Like mosquitoes, they would always find your tender spots. Ultimately, we could not avoid meeting the enemy, eye to eye in our bedroom!

3

CHILDHOOD IN OUR ANCESTRAL VILLAGE

Surviving childhood was not easy at any time in Chinese history, particularly in wartime. I spent nearly four years of my childhood in Nam Bin, the village of my forefathers. Although we were able to live in a half-decent house of solid bricks inherited from my grandfather, it did not have any lights, bathrooms, or running water. Our ancestral house was considered at that time the biggest and best dwelling in a village that was made up mostly of mud houses. It had four one-bedroom apartments facing a central courtyard, and looked old and primitive compared to my father's modern Western-styled house in the city of Canton, built in 1928. My father and his three brothers each owned one unit in the old house, built in the 1890s. Each apartment consisted of a large bedroom and a kitchen, and children slept in the same room with their parents. I shared my bed with my mother.

Our house had been constructed in the latter part of the nineteenth century by our grandfather Yuk Goh, who had inherited considerable wealth from our great-grandfather Gim Sing, a prosperous farmer and landowner. Unfortunately, my grandfather squandered his inherited fortune, because of his addiction to opium. My father and his three brothers had to fend for themselves, and look for opportunities far from home.

The old house looked spooky when I first set foot in it, because there was only one small window in each room, with dark shadows everywhere. I liked the courtyard, because it was bright and airy. At the back of the courtyard was a shallow wooden shelf about thirty inches wide. Tablets bearing the names and photos of my grandparents stood on this ledge. I used to stay in the open courtyard as much as possible to avoid going inside our dark bedroom alone, because village kids had told me that there were headless ghosts lurking in every dark corner, ready to pounce and snatch my head away.

Our apartment was empty when we moved in. My mother had to buy a bed made with wooden planks, a mosquito net, kitchen utensils, and other essentials. She tried to find employment, but could not. She was forced to sell goods such as salted fish, fermented bean curd, and any other bits as a street peddler, so we would not starve. She and my aunt Sai Sum usually worked together, both for companionship and safety. Every day at dawn, I could see my mother hoisting a bamboo pole over her shoulder, with two baskets loaded with goods on each end. She would then briskly walk out of the house, to sell at the local market or sometimes to go from village to village. Just before sundown, she would return home to cook us bits of rice mixed with corn, yam, squash, or pumpkin as fillers. A small sliver of salted fish the size of my thumb, or a cube of fermented tofu, would give some taste to the bland food. Whenever my mother was late coming home, my stomach would growl and I would start to worry: was she all right? Maybe she had been caught by the Japanese or robbed by bandits? Thank God, she never failed to come home, although sometimes it was well after the sun had set, because she had to sell the last of her goods or dodge the Japanese patrols. Occasionally she came home with a delightful surprise: meat!

A few times a year, I would jump for joy when I smelled the fragrance of a piece of barbecued pork or a leg of chicken. It would be combined with a full bowl of rice, not mixed with hateful fillers such as corn and yam, which were not the sweet varieties that we enjoy in North America. Whenever we had decent meat, I felt I was in heaven, because those times were so infrequent, being limited to Chinese New Year and special occasions, such as birthdays. All through those years in the village, I do not remember getting invited to a banquet of any kind, not a wedding or a baby's Full Month birthday celebration, for villagers were poor and times were uncertain. I still remember one chicken leg on my birthday lasted me for three days, as my mother steamed one portion of the leg again and again for three meals, with some salty fish sauce each dinner. Two meals a day did not fill the belly of a growing boy; I felt hungry all the time. On several occasions, I stole a few tangerines, sweet potatoes, and sugar cane from nearby farms, my stomach overpowering the shame and the risk of being caught.

I still remember the Ching Ming Festival in the spring of 1944; it was an occasion to honour our ancestors by visiting their graves, and an opportunity for some meat that day. I had looked forward to this festival, because my mother and neighbours had told me that a roasted pig and burning incense would be offered to the revered ancestors of our clan, and, after the ceremony, the pig would be chopped up and distributed to all the families. On that day, I went eagerly with a soup bowl to the village hall and received in my bowl two slices the size of my little hands. The golden-brown meat and the aroma were so mouth-watering that I immediately started gobbling it. When I reached home, only a small piece the size of my two fingers was left. Ashamed of my gluttonous behaviour, I dared not look into my mother's eyes as she took the bowl from me. I expected a tongue-lashing or worse, but she only hugged me and asked if I wanted any more. I shook my head and wrapped my arms around her.

A little later, my throat and stomach began to feel engorged and extremely uncomfortable, as if a cork had stuck in my throat. I tried repeatedly to throw up to relieve the agony, but to no avail. My mother came to my aid by putting her middle finger deeply into my mouth and tickling the back of my palate; finally, I was able to expel the partially digested pork. This incident taught me to never overeat, especially rich food on an empty stomach!

With the adults at work, I was alone in the house most of the time, although my mother had asked Dung Sew, a young woman a few doors from us, to check on me occasionally. Every morning, before she left the house, my mother instructed me not to venture out too far, not to play with fire, and not to swim or fight. Sometimes I forgot and waded into the fish pond in front of our house to cool off in the summer. On one occasion, I stepped into a hole and disappeared under the water, but luckily my cousin Suey Way was there to grab me. On another occasion, I caught some grasshoppers and a big spider and roasted them over a small fire that I built outside our house with dried bamboo leaves and twigs. Since I had not tasted meat for many days, these insects were delicious. However, I got infected with parasitic worms in my intestines, and had to drink many bowls of foul-tasting Chinese herbs to get rid of my infestation.

Living in a poor rural village was a very difficult adjustment for a city-born child like me. I disliked having to wear thin, black cloth shoes – or worse, going barefoot – instead of enjoying comfortable leather shoes. Often, I stepped barefooted on chicken droppings, cow dung, or dog droppings. Even after my feet had a thorough washing, the odour still clung to my toes.

I loathed the outdoor washrooms. They were dark, windowless latrines, without seats, water, or electricity. These facilities were located in another part of the village, and were owned by some farmers. They used the smelly excrement as fertilizer, as their forefathers had done since the time of the "Yellow Emperor," who was an ancient legend. When I had to go into one of those suffocating cubbyholes, I would try to hold my breath, do my business, and jump out, before my pants were fully pulled up. It was so much nicer to sit on a portable bucket at home, particularly on cold or rainy days. But every morning Mother had to lug the bucket out to empty it into a farmer's latrine.

Most of the dogs in the village ran free, and I noticed that two of them ate human feces. In fact, I often saw one particular child squat in an open space, pull down his pants, and pooh on the ground. His dog would run over to lap up the excrement. One day I was feeling naughty and decided to experiment with his dog. When I saw it snooping around our front door, I went out behind a tree and poohed. It ate my offering with relish!

A nearby river served as the source of our drinking water and as our main bathtub, whenever the weather was not too cold. Yellow leeches were always lurking in the water, and they seemed to love my blood type. I used a little bucket to carry water home, to help my mother, although I was told not to. No one had ever taught me how to swim.

Mother worked six to seven days a week, going out at dawn and coming home at dusk. To help Mother prepare dinner faster, I would gather some leaves and twigs from a nearby bamboo grove to use for cooking on the hearth. Before I was seven, Mother stored hot water in a thermos bottle for me to drink. After that, she taught me to boil water and make tea. I was warned never to drink any water without boiling it first, to avoid diarrhea or something worse.

The village kids were not very friendly, because I was not one of them, and I spoke the village dialect rather badly. I did have fun whenever Cousin Ho Gor was home, but he was away most of the time. I played by myself or with Suey Lung and Suey Way, cousins who shared our ancestral house. They were sons of my Third Uncle: Albert (Suey Lung) and David (Suey Way). Albert was closest to me in age, one and a half years older, but, unfortunately, he liked to bully me and was the least likable of all my cousins, so I only played with him when there were no other boys around.

Suey Way was several years older than I, and we got along very well, because he was gentle and protective of me. He was skinny and small in stature, but not in courage. He was disadvantaged further because he had been adopted from Canada by Third Uncle, who brought him to China for Third Aunt to raise as her own, because she had a daughter but not a son at that time. He was of mixed blood, half-Chinese and half-white. Village kids taunted him and called him Foreign Devil Kid. He fought his tormentors tenaciously, however overmatched he might have been. More than a few times I saw him with bruises or a bloody nose.

As for schooling, my mother could not afford it when food was critical for our survival. However, at the age of seven, I did go to the school in a neighbouring village for one term of about three months.

I had not wanted to go to school because I was still feeling strange with the other children of the village, who were rough country kids. Somewhat afraid of them, I resisted with all my might my mother's entreaties, but she finally prevailed. She spent several late nights making black pants and white cotton shirts for me, cutting the cloth from her own old city clothes. Because my leather shoes had long worn out, I wore my black cloth shoes, which were particularly uncomfortable when they got wet on rainy, muddy days.

Mother took a rare day off work to drag me to meet the teacher, Mr. Chou. I stood for a long time trying to listen to his many rules, most of which I could not understand because of his dialect. The first thing that he tried to teach me was how to write my name, which in Chinese characters is very complicated, in that it involves more than forty strokes. It took me several days of repetitive writing and copying with first a pencil and then a brush to learn to write my name legibly.

The classroom was a large room that held over thirty-five boys of varying ages. Most days we spent learning Chinese characters, copying and writing with a fine brush dipped in ink that we made ourselves by pouring a half-spoonful of water into a small bowl and then grinding a stick of black chalk into the water at the bottom of the bowl. I had to grind it over a hundred times until the ink became thick enough to write with. One morning I was a bit lazy and sleepy, and my ink ran all over the thin rice paper; there was no resemblance to legible characters. My punishment was to thicken the ink some more and to write each character again a hundred times. On another occasion, I misunderstood my assignment, and the teacher strapped me on both palms with a bamboo stick. I tried to hide the welts from my mother. She did not notice them until dinner time, when she saw that I was handling my chopsticks awkwardly. I was forced to open my hands and explain. She gave me a tongue lashing, but the disappointment on her face remained with me far longer than my physical pain.

Our schooling was interrupted time and again because we had to flee from the Japanese. The soldiers were camped at a nearby town, and they often searched the surrounding villages for able-bodied men for their labour – and, of course, for women and girls. With the interruptions and different ages and indifferent attitudes of the boys, there was very little learning. My mother could afford only one term for me at this school, because she was often sick and could not work. It was inauspicious and not very productive, but I did learn how to write my name with a brush and make ink, and I acquired some appreciation of Chinese calligraphy. Anything else I forgot quickly, except the strapping, which remained vivid in my memory.

In our village, I befriended a big water buffalo called Big Ox. He lumbered past our house every day, looking at me with bemused eyes and a wagging tail. I loved to pat his dark, leathery flank, and in response, on a couple of occasions, he dropped a massive, smelly load near my feet. However, I still liked this rascal, and wanted very much to ride him. His owner, Uncle Tong, rarely allowed anyone to do that, but once he gave in to my begging and hoisted me onto the back of Big Ox, took off his straw hat, and plopped it down on my head. With me sitting proudly astride his beast, he led us towards the fish pond for its bath. Several children watched me with envy, and called me Little Ox.

Starvation and diseases wrecked many lives in our village. An entire family of five living a few doors from us perished. In addition, several young men were abducted by the Japanese for slave labour in their armies, digging ditches and carrying heavy weapons. Most of them were never heard from again. Every day could have been our last on earth, but by the grace of God, somehow we survived, but not without deep scars.

4

AN ENEMY IN MY BED

On a chilly, sombre day in the winter of 1944, I had a terrifyingly close encounter with an enemy in Xin Hui. I was seven years old and sick in bed with a fever. My mother and I were alone in our house, and she was cajoling me to drink some foul-smelling, bitter-tasting black medicinal tea, when suddenly there was uproar outside. People were shouting as they ran by our house: "The Japs are coming! The Japs are here! Run! Run!"

My mother's hands shook and drops of dark liquid spilled on my pyjamas before she ran out to look. She dashed back to grab me off the bed, which was made with wooden boards laid between two wooden benches. She shoved aside some junk from under the bed, and pushed me ahead of her on my elbows and knees to the farthest and darkest corner of the space. She rearranged old suitcases and bags to hide us, but I could see through little gaps. We huddled in this dark and musty cocoon, where cobwebs stuck to my nose and mouth. Keeping very still, I sensed some little creatures scurrying around us. Shrinking into a ball, I prayed that those rodents wouldn't lick me.

Soon we heard shouting in strange dialects and banging at the door of the building's main entrance. For several minutes, the thick wooden door was battered savagely. Then we heard noise up on our roof and someone jumped into our central courtyard from the open skylight. Our heavy door squeaked and groaned open, and men poured in, causing panic and frantic squealing from my little pet pig of six weeks. Bang! A shot rang out and for several long seconds my piglet screamed, it's oinking loud and shrill. My mother clamped her hand over my mouth to stifle my sobs; I stuck my fingers into my ears.

I squinted in the darkness and saw a soldier come into our bedroom. He stood still and looked around. We lay deathly quiet as his heavy boots thumped on the earthen floor, coming directly towards us. He stopped by the bed, and I saw a long sword dangling beside his tall leather boots. For an instant, I thought I saw a pair of eyes peeking in at me. I peed in my pants. Just then another voice hollered from the doorway, and the first soldier turned and marched out.

Pots and pans were rattling from the kitchen located just outside our bedroom. A cacophony of noises filled the air – chopping, talking, and laughing, with the occasional smashing of dishes. Quietly, I wept, because I knew the poor piglet I had raised since it was weaned from its mother was no more. I prayed that these Eastern Devils would soon finish eating and leave, but then a soldier entered our room again and staggered towards us. At the bedside, a wooden bucket was kicked and the lid clanged noisily. Luckily, the bucket that had served as our portable toilet had been emptied earlier that morning. He stood by the bed, so close that the odour of cow dung on his boots assailed my nose. Our wooden bed shook and creaked as he sat down on it. For several minutes, all was eerily quiet. The silence was terrifying. My heart pounded madly in my chest.

Soon we heard grunting. I didn't dare stretch, and my legs were cramped and hurting. My pants felt wet, sticky, and smelly. The intruder mumbled incoherently and snored, only inches from my head. I remained curled up, breathing stealthily through my mouth. My head ached terribly and my throat tickled; I was so afraid that I might cough.

Half an hour might have gone by before another soldier marched into the room, yelled something, clicked his heels, and went out quickly. My "bed-mate" stirred and grunted. He rose from his slumber and stumbled out of the room. We waited, while our eyes and ears strained in the semi-darkness. When all had been quiet for some time, my mother crawled out slowly from our hiding place. Minutes later, she came back to help me slither out. Pins and needles shot up my legs as I tried to stand up, and I half-leaned on my mother as I walked out of the room.

The sights in our kitchen and courtyard were horrific. Blood, guts, and bones were all over the place. The head of my beloved little pig sat obscenely on the chopping board, with blood congealed on its snout. I turned to hide my head in my mother's lap, as a fresh burst of tears came upon me. My mother then sat me down on my wooden stool, gave me a rice biscuit and a cup of hot water from our thermos, and told me to stay put as she went out to check on the neighbours. Later, my older cousins told me that an auntie, a few doors away, had been battered and raped.

On that horrible day, Mother and I considered ourselves very lucky to have escaped the fate that befell my piglet; but we lost all of our precious supply of rice, yams, and cooking oil. What they could not use for cooking their lunch, they took away. These losses would contribute heavily to my mother's near-fatal illness from malnutrition and anaemia a few months later. After I had calmed down a bit that evening, Mother touched my forehead and thought that I was running a fever. She tucked me back into my bed, which reeked of a strange odour.

Looking up at my mother's pale, sad face, I asked, "Where is BaBa? Can you write to him to get us away from this place?" She answered that BaBa was far away in Toronto, because his last letter had been from Canada more than three years before, at about the time the Japanese bombed Pearl Harbor. Since then, mail across the Pacific Ocean had stopped entirely. She told me not to ask any more questions but to rest. She had to clean up and salvage what food was left by those Eastern Devils.

The saddest part for me was losing my beloved piglet. At dinner I could not eat, as I watched my mother slowly chewing on the tiny leg of my pet. Tears rolled down both of our faces. I was shell-shocked, and my hatred for these terrible oppressors grew.

Nonetheless, the full horror of the war would not hit me until later, after Japan had surrendered. I saw photographs in a news magazine about the Nanjing Massacre of 1937, when the Japanese Imperial Army captured that city. Over two hundred thousand civilians were reportedly massacred. One picture was particularly traumatic to my young mind: it showed a nude woman lying on the ground, a bayonet stuck in her belly just above her dark patch of hair, and the twisted body of a child lying on her breast. An enemy soldier stood nearby, with a crazed smirk on his face and the pompous air of a conquering hero.

After seeing these graphic images, I started having nightmares; I dreamt that:

> I saw my mother and I were discovered by the soldier in my bed when a coughing spell burst from my throat. He yelled and brandished his sword, flushing us out of our lair. He slapped my mother, threw her on the bed and began tearing away her clothes. My fist flailed at him and he kicked me, sending me sprawling to the wall. Inevitably, I would wake up screaming and with my pyjamas soaking wet.

5

EIGHT BUSHELS OF RICE

My mother and I faced many desperate times in 1944 and 1945, a sequence of despair. My mother and I shared our ancestral home in Xin Hui with Third Aunt, Fourth Aunt, and their children. Fourth Aunt and her son Ho Gor were my favourite relatives. She and my mother were best of friends and sisters-in-law. I called her Sai Sum

During those years, many mornings we woke up hungry and cursed the Japanese. Mother fell seriously ill because of malnutrition and the constant stress living under Japanese occupation. Her legs became swollen like a thick squash and she could hardly walk. She shuffled slowly around the house or sat in bed, looking grim and distraught. I laid my head on her lap, bewildered.

A distant relative I called Auntie Kei Sum came to visit us, bringing with her a small bag of rice, a few eggs, and Chinese sausages. For dinner, my mother cooked this food, not the poor fare in our house. The meal was the best I had tasted in over four years, ever since December 1941, when we fled Hong Kong. Auntie Kei Sum said that I was looking pale, scrawny, and too small for an eight-year-old. As we were drinking tea after eating, Auntie Kei Sum stroked my face and pinched my arm and exclaimed: "Ah Lun is too thin, not much flesh on him. He must eat more!" She wanted to talk to my mother privately, so Mother sent me out to play. Later, she told me about their conversation. Aunty Kei Sum was childless; she wanted to adopt me. She said further that, with the war dragging on, Mother and I might not survive. She offered my mother eight bushels of rice, one for each year that Mother had raised me, and a promise that she would feed me rice every day.

That evening, Mother, with tears rolling down her face, told me more about our desperate circumstances. She said that I would be well fed at Auntie Kei Sum's house. She held my hands tightly as we talked, sitting at our small kitchen table. I vowed that I would not go; I would rather starve and die with her. We clung to each other. She whispered that, if she gave me away, she would not be able to face my father some day, whether in this life or in the spirit world. Again, I asked her why BaBa couldn't come to help us, and again she explained that the Japanese navy had stopped all shipping coming to China, and we had not received any rental money from our properties in Canton, because the tenants had all fled. We cried until we were exhausted and fell asleep, my body curled against her bony ribs. When I woke up to pee, I discovered that she was still weeping; she got up to help me find the chamber pot in our dark room.

The next morning Mother complained that she felt weak and woozy and told me to ask Sai Sum to cook breakfast. Auntie was alarmed and came immediately to our room. She urged Mother to see a doctor as soon as possible. When Auntie went to prepare the morning meal of rice and squash, she saw that our rice bin was nearly empty. She went to Third Aunt's kitchen and borrowed two large bowls of rice, enough for a couple of days. Third Aunt was luckier than us because her parents were able to help her occasionally.

Two days later, Mother was able to walk a little better. Sai Sum solicited the help of Third Aunt, Lan Ying, and together they persuaded Mother to see a doctor. With my aunts supporting her, my mother was able to slowly make her way to the town of Dai Jak, about two miles away.

My mother and aunts went to the clinic of a Dr. Lui. He gave my mother an injection and some medicine to take home, and told her that her illness was caused by severe malnutrition. She must eat more and better food, particularly rice with the red skins intact. After paying the doctor for the visit and some medicine, she had enough money left for only a couple of pounds of a coarse, inferior brand of rice, in which some dirt was still visible. While they were standing at the shop figuring out how much more rice they could buy if all three of them emptied their pockets, a woman they were acquainted with saw them and stopped to talk.

Mrs. Lum lived two villages away from us. Her husband was a "sojourner" like my father, owner of a laundry in Toronto. Speaking the same Xin Hui dialect and being so far away from their native land, Mr. Wong and my father naturally had become close friends. When Mrs. Wong learned about my mother's illness and sensed that my mother and aunts were unable to purchase more than a few pounds of rice, she offered to lend my mother a bushel of rice that she had in storage at home. Putting aside her pride, my mother gratefully accepted.

Thanks to Mrs. Lum's generosity and kindness, together with the help of my two aunts, Dr. Lui's medicine, and a lot of garlic eaten daily, along with fervent prayers to the Goddess Quan Yin, my mother began to recover.

Coincidentally, two days after Kei Sum's visit, Cousin Ho Gor came home from his work somewhere far away. He told us that America had begun firebombing Tokyo, and that the United States had developed some stupendous bombs, ready to be dropped on Japan. 'This war should end soon," he declared. With renewed hope, resolve and feeling a little stronger, my mother rejected her offer to adopt me.

China's "Eight Years War of Resistance" came to a merciful end when Japan agreed to surrender unconditionally on August 15, 1945. Firecrackers exploded everywhere in our village. After a couple of days of frenzy and joyful delirium, we began to pick up the shattered pieces of our lives. For several weeks, while their soldiers were waiting for repatriation to their homeland, I saw in the town of Dai Jak several forlorn-looking Japanese soldiers, who were working on collecting garbage and sweeping the roads. I joined the children in taunting them. At last we had a chance to vent our anger and hatred by calling them vile names. They kept silent with their heads down while we jeered at them.

On September 3, the Japanese foreign minister and several generals, representing Japan's armed forces, officially signed the document of surrender to General Douglas MacArthur on the deck of the battleship USS *Missouri*. A few days later, a couple of men from our village went with a regiment of Chinese Nationalist soldiers to the Japanese garrison that was stationed in our county. The enemies were disarmed. One villager said he threw garbage at them and slapped the captain, the way he himself was often slapped during the occupation.

The fact that I survived this period of my childhood was truly a miracle. With time, maturity, and spirituality, I would heal and I always appreciated that my mother refused to trade me for eight bushels of rice.

6

DEATH OF A BELOVED BANDIT

People had called him a Communist bandit, a hero, and a martyr. His full name was Chow Lai Ho. (In Chinese, family names come before given names.) I called him Ho Gor in Cantonese, meaning Elder Brother Ho. He was my favourite cousin, nine years older than me, son of Fourth Uncle and Sai Sum. He often played with me, told me stories, taught me to draw, and sometimes gave me candies.

When we all moved from the city to our ancestral village in Xin Hui, Ho Gor had had to stop his schooling. Most of the time he could not find any steady work, only odd jobs like reading and writing letters for illiterate farmers. They might pay him with some sweet potatoes, a few eggs, or a small chicken, not enough to last for even a week. Like my mother and me, he too suffered hunger and malnutrition. He went away two years before the end of the war, coming home only occasionally, maybe once every few months, staying one night, and departing early the next morning. He usually brought home some food. Mother and I always looked forward to seeing Ho Gor, because he and Sai Sum shared their goodies with us, allaying our hunger for a few days.

One evening at bedtime, after he had read to me some English folk tales in Chinese, about Robin Hood and his Merry Men, I asked him what he was doing when he went away so much. Couldn't he stay another day? He answered that he worked as a reporter for a newspaper, which meant constantly travelling, and sometimes even having to fight the Japanese in guerilla warfare. He said the war should end soon, because he had heard that the United States had invented some hugely lethal bombs and was going to drop some on Japan. He declared further that justice would soon be done to Japanese collaborators, greedy landowners, and capricious Guomindang warlords and Chiang Kai-shek. I informed him that a couple of the villagers had called him a Commie Bandit behind his back.

I asked him, "Ho Gor, are you a Commie Bandit? Where did you get the food you brought home today?"

"From some people that I know," my cousin replied. "Remember a while back I told you the stories from a famous Chinese novel *Heroes of the Water Margin*? The stories are very similar to the ones I told you tonight about the Englishman Robin Hood. Well, recently we acquired some food from a few big landowners and gave it to many starving people. Isn't this a good thing?"

"Yes. Are you a Chinese Robin Hood?" I inquired further.

He shrugged his shoulders, tucked me in, and said, "No more questions. Sleep now."

As soon as Japan surrendered and world peace was proclaimed in the summer of 1945, civil war started again between Mao Zedong's Communists and Chiang Kai-shek's Guomindang, each party wanting to control all of China. My mother and Ho Gor's mother, Sai Sum, were planning to wind up their affairs and leave the village. It was time for us to return to Canton to rebuild our lives, and for me to start formal schooling. However, Ho Gor had not come home for a long time, and we could not leave without him. There was no way for us to contact him, so we waited anxiously.

One rainy night, I was brushing my teeth with a bit of salt on my well-worn toothbrush, when our big wooden front door squeaked open. Ho Gor slipped in very quietly. He greeted Mother with a quick "Ney ho ma" and hurried to his mother's room. I immediately rinsed my mouth and ran to look for him. The door was ajar when I peeked in. He and Sai Sum were stuffing things into a black linen bag. When he was changing his shirt, I saw a gun holster with bullets and a pistol. My eyes widened but, before I could speak, he pushed past me, saying only "I have to run. Be good."

Sai Sum was sitting on the edge of her bed, her head bowed and her hands covering her face. I asked what was the matter and why Ho Gor was not staying the night. She didn't explain. She told me to go to bed.

My mother was tucking me under my blanket when Bang, Bang, Bang, three shots rang out. A moment later we heard shouting outside, followed by loud knocking. When my mother and Sai Sum went to investigate, four soldiers rushed into our courtyard, swearing and demanding loudly, "Where is the Commie Bandit Chow Lai Ho?" Mother and Sai Sum could not answer them, so they quickly searched the rooms. One soldier yanked me out of bed and shook me by my shoulders, asking questions, while another pointed his gun at me. I peed in my pajamas.

For weeks afterwards, we were all very nervous and constantly looked over our shoulders. My mother told me those unsavoury soldiers who pursued Ho Gor and threatened us worked for a local warlord who was working for Chiang Kai-shek, and who wanted to eliminate all Communists or perceived Communists. Civil wars erupted all over China.

One late evening, in the fall of 1945, we heard soft knocking. When Sai Sum opened the front door, she found two young persons in black, wearing large bamboo hats. She quickly took the man and woman to her room. Moments later we heard sobbing, and Mother and I rushed to see why Sai Sum was crying? The youthful couple told us that they were comrades of Chow Lai Ho. A few days before, a group of Guomindang soldiers had ambushed them, and a fierce battle ensued. Lai Ho was captured and shot by soldiers of Chiang Kai-shek. As the visitors hurried to depart, they urged Mother and me to take care of Sai Sum. They left behind a few dollars.

Sai Sum cried day and night, and stayed in bed all the time, refusing to eat or to go out with my mother. She kept saying she wanted to die, that she had no more hope now that she had lost all her children. Mother had told me that Sai Sum's two other sons had died from malnutrition and disease earlier in the Japanese occupation. When I brought her tea and a bowl of rice congee, she shook her head. Her face was ravaged by tears of grief. I cried with her, because she was like a second mother to me, and I was her favourite nephew. After two to three days of our pleading and begging, she finally took a little food and hot water. Mother and I had hidden all the knives and scissors, for fear she would try to kill herself. For several nights, we slept in her bed with her. I went everywhere with her, even waiting outside the smelly outhouse. Somehow, we managed to save her, and she lived for many more years.

7

CRIES FOR JUSTICE

After the Japanese surrender, we awaited redress and reparations. We all wanted revenge on our brutal enemies. They had killed and maimed millions of us, and my mother nearly got raped and forced to be a "comfort woman" for their troops. Japanese soldiers raped and regularly kidnapped women and girls to service them sexually.

A relative, Hung Lok, who was attending college and read the newspapers regularly, kept us up-to-date on what was happening in the world, particularly news about the Japanese War Crime Tribunals, organized by the United States, with input from China, Great Britain, Russia, the Philippines, Australia, and other allies. The American Supreme Commander for the Far East, General Douglas MacArthur, had total control of this tribunal and of postwar Japan. The millions of living victims, including my mother and me, hoped that justice would soon be rendered.

To our dismay, we heard very little news. Hardly anyone was punished; certainly not war criminals such as the mastermind of the Nanjing Massacre, General Matsui, or General Tojo, the prime minister of Japan from 1941 to 1944. Even with the urgent pleas of China, the Philippines, and other Allied powers, the Americans had not put Emperor Hirohito on trial. How much did this head of state of the Japanese Empire know about the brutal colonization of Korea, the invasion of China, the attacks on Pearl Harbor and on other countries? Did he authorize these attacks? If not, did he do anything to prevent or stop such atrocious aggression? General MacArthur did not question this "Divine Emperor," and personally gave him immunity. Why?

Speculation was that the general wanted to spare the emperor, who would help him to rule Japan peacefully, because most Japanese had held the emperor in the highest esteem. His overthrow or execution would arouse rebellion and guerrilla warfare against the Americans. Of special concern were the kamikazes, who might try to assassinate American officials in suicide attacks.

In recent years, I have learned much more about postwar Japan and MacArthur's handling of the war tribunals, particularly from American author James Bradley's meticulously researched book *Fly Boys*. This eminent writer has a great deal to say about the Japanese military and their barbaric treatment of the defeated – especially of American pilots who were shot down and captured. Some American POWs were beheaded; a few were even cannibalized.

The Chinese were anxious to put another arch-villain on trial. This was Surgeon General Ishii, the mastermind of the chemical and germ warfare programs in northern China. He used innocent civilians and POWs as guinea pigs in experiments with biological agents, such as cholera, anthrax, botulism, and mustard gas. Other atrocities included vivisections: a gruesome medical technique of cutting up a live person, so that the young military doctors could practise their surgical skills. Over half a million victims were killed, mostly Chinese, but other nationalities as well, including some American POWs. They died horrible deaths, suffering much longer and more hideously than if they had been shot. Ishii was a most wanted man, dead or alive, but he disappeared into hiding as soon as Japan surrendered.

The American high command looked for him, anxious to extract his knowledge and experimental data on chemical and biological warfare. The Americans and the Russians were also doing research in this field, although to a lesser extent. Eventually, Ishii came out of hiding. However, he was not put on trial, and the Chinese were greatly puzzled and disappointed. Apparently, this monster negotiated a plea bargain with General MacArthur: he would not be prosecuted in return for giving all his experimental data to the Americans. What injustice to the dead!

Finally, on December 23, 1948, General Tojo, General Matsui, and five other Class A war criminals were executed by hanging in Tokyo. We rejoiced, feeling a small measure of justice was done, but many more war criminals should have been punished, for they had killed and maimed millions. We had waited for more than three years, and only a handful were executed. Emperor Hirohito was barely touched, although he had to renounce his divinity and give up most of his authority to an elected assembly and a prime minister.

To this day, Japan has not apologized or paid any reparations to the Chinese and others. In contrast, the German government has acknowledged the Holocaust, apologized, paid some reparations to the victims of the Nazis, and prosecuted a number of Nazi war criminals, even though many escaped punishment.

Where is justice? The Japanese have consistently downplayed their atrocities and the actual number of people they killed. They labelled as prostitutes the women and girls they kidnapped and used as "comfort women." The soldiers looked down on the people they conquered as inferior, not worthy of their respect. The Chinese have felt this injustice keenly. In fact, it is a source of friction between China and Japan to this day. Furthermore, Japanese history textbooks have mentioned very little about Japanese aggression, but have portrayed the Japanese as victims. They focused on their suffering from the atomic bombs dropped on Hiroshima and Nagasaki, and the firebombing of their cities, which destroyed millions of homes, most of which were constructed of wood and paper. Large numbers of their citizens were burned to death. I certainly have sympathy for those poor, innocent Japanese, but not for the inhumane militarists.

The vast majority of Japanese born after 1950 do not know that their nation invaded other countries. Full reconciliation will not happen until Japan owns up to the crimes against humanity committed in the twentieth century. Japan's consistent refusal to admit guilt has impoverished its culture. Many Asians still harbour a lasting mistrust of Japan, particularly as they see the rise of militarism and rearmament in recent years. In refusing to face its past, Japan has lost much of the moral foundation that was once hers.

Fortunately, there are a small number of courageous Japanese, including some veterans who served in the wars in China, Korea, the Philippines, and other places, who have confessed to their horrible deeds. I have seen books and documentary films made by Japanese citizens who are honest and brave enough to tell the truth. They have done so at considerable risk to themselves, because the ultra-nationalists threaten those who dare to speak out.

The Japanese people generally are good and cultured, but in the Second World War, their soldiers were sadistic and arrogant, with a few exceptions. They looked down on people they subjugated as subhuman, raping women and children by the tens of thousands, and often bayoneting them to death afterwards. Their military were unbelievably inhumane, burying prisoners-of-war and innocent people alive, chopping off heads, or shooting masses of them with machine guns. I do not believe those soldiers were born evil, but because of circumstances and brainwashing, they committed those beastly deeds.

Philosophically speaking, I have come to realize that the evils of the Second World War were perpetuated by some Fascists, warmongers, and nationalistic fanatics. I think that any nation or people can be capable of cruel acts of inhumanity, as shown clearly by Hitler and his Nazis, Stalin and his Communists, numerous brutal dictators, and many others.

I have realized that, in order to live a healthy life, I must accept my karma; I started to cultivate compassion and forgiveness to free myself from the past. I do not wish to be hounded by bitterness and hatred, but I also want to speak out against Japan's government for whitewashing their war crimes. I am aware that millions of innocent Japanese also suffered from the Second World War: conscripted soldiers sent into the war and victims of the atomic bombs and Americans' firebombing of their homes near the end of the war. Tens of thousands good men, women, and children died from starvation, all due to the reckless folly of the militarists. I still cannot fully comprehend how the Japanese military could be so inhumane, when all the Japanese I have personally met in peacetime in Japan and North America have been decent and kind, including my niece Holly's husband and many friends and dental colleagues of Japanese heritage.

Recently, Archbishop Desmond Tutu was quoted as saying, in the publication *The Book of Joy*, "An eye for an eye will leave the whole world blind." We have had enough wars and killings all over the globe; we do not need any more hatred and revenge. My hope is that all nations and their citizens have twenty-twenty vision: be forgiving and live life with joy and respect for other people and traditions. After all, is there any other good option?

In Canada, Dr. Joseph Wong founded Toronto ALPHA. It is an educational, non-profit charity that promotes historical investigation of the events of World War II in Asia. The aim is to foster reconciliation, healing and cross-cultural understanding.

INTERLUDE 1945–49

The jubilation of victory and the end of the war was very short-lived for us, because of the death of Cousin Lai Ho. In late November 1945, my mother and I gladly took leave of our village, to return to our home in the city of Canton. We had to take Sai Sum away from the killing fields of Xin Hui, and I had to start formal schooling. With peace restored, we also hoped fervently that my father would soon return to see us.

Arriving back to the city of my birth, we found that our detached, solid-brick house was still standing, but in an unlivable condition, with gaping bomb holes and all the doors and windows shattered. Everything inside the home was gone; there were not even pipes or a toilet. Mother and Sai Sum were devastated, because we had no place to live. Luckily, our good friends Grandma Leen Tong and her family, the Lees, took us in to live in their three-storey home. My father sent us American dollars, and my mother began to rebuild our house, which took more than six months, because there was a severe shortage of building supplies.

The Lees' building was a large structure near a river, and from the garden we had a fine view of a tributary of the mighty Pearl River. Their house was in decent shape, with minimal damage, because high-ranking Japanese officers had lived in it, returning it to the Lees at the end of the war. The front garden was large, and Sai Sum, my mother, and the Lees grew vegetables. We harvested green beans, snow peas, mustard greens, and sweet corn.

There was a junior school to which I could walk in fifteen minutes, and it accepted me into Grade 1, even though at age eight I hardly knew anything, except how to write my name. In addition, I had forgotten my city dialect of Canton and spoke only the village dialect of Xin Hui, so I had difficulty understanding the lessons. However, after six months, in the summer of 1946, I was confident enough to sit for the entrance examinations to Pui Ching Elementary School, known as the best private school in the city, founded by American Baptists. Christianity was taught weekly, and each year a big religious rally would be held for conversion to Christ. Although my mother was a lifetime Buddhist, she had no objection to my going to Pui Ching, because of its gold-standard reputation, and because Grandma Leen Tong, a devout Baptist, had strongly recommended it to her.

In Grade 1, I did very well and was ranked first in my class in deportment and academics. Miss Pang, my teacher, encouraged me to try the Grade 3 entrance exams in order to skip Grade 2, and to my surprise I was successful. Grade 3 and Grade 4 were much more challenging, but I was learning a lot of interesting subjects, especially History, Geography, and Chinese and English literature (the latter in translation, of course). I was not able to achieve top ranking any more, neither in Grade 3 or Grade 4, although I won first prize in a General Knowledge contest in Grade 4.

Physical education at school was an important part of our curriculum; I enjoyed calisthenics, Ping-Pong, soccer, and basketball. Track-and-field competitions took up nearly a week each year. I participated in the hundred-yard dash and the high jump, but did not win any ribbons, although at five feet, two inches tall at age twelve, I could jump five feet, one inch.

Emerging from the Second World War, China was poor and backward. Leisure activities, games and sports, were very limited when I was going to school. Television was unheard of, and most homes like ours did not have a telephone. New technology was developing very slowly, though nothing like it has in the past fifty years. Most of my friends and I collected stamps as a hobby. I would trade my Canadian stamps with other boys, some of whom had fathers working in the United States, Cuba, Southeast Asia, Australia, and other parts of the world. By studying my stamps, I learned much about the geography, history, and culture of many countries. Where is New Zealand? Who is Napoleon? What is an Egyptian pyramid? I often asked my teachers, especially the librarian.

My friends and I kept active mentally and physically. None of us was fat. We played soccer, basketball, Ping-Pong, and marbles, and ran around playing Soldiers and Bandits. Other activities that I particularly liked were kite fighting, kikbo, and reading.

Kite flying is very popular in China, particularly in the spring, when the sun is warm and the wind is favourable. My friends and I went to parks and open spaces, sometimes on the flat roofs of our houses, to fly kites of all sizes, shapes, and colours. After I had gained some proficiency, I then tried kite fighting, because it was more thrilling, challenging, and had more at stake. Each participant's objective was to force an opponent to surrender and quit, or to cut loose his kite and set it adrift. Each of my kites might cost the same as going to two movies.

Unfortunately, I was not skillful and lost much more often than I won, particularly to Cousin Suey Lung, my former bully, who lived in our house in 1948 and 1949. I begged him to teach me his techniques and, for the price of six American stamps from my collection, he gave me three lessons on how to sweep, spin, lift, and manoeuvre my kite to get on top of my opponent's string and sever it. After that, I did a little better against other boys, but had no success at all against my cousin. Then, one day, I came home early and found Suey Lung soaking his strings in a mixture of glue and finely ground glass. At last, I had discovered his secret! Afraid of cutting my fingers and not crazy for such tactics, I gave up kite fighting and played more table tennis and kikbo.

Ping-Pong, or table tennis, was played in nearly all the schools, even those poorest schools without a gymnasium or schoolyard. In China at that time, very few schools were publicly funded. My mother had to pay high tuition at my school, because of its reputation. Thus, we had very good classroom and sports facilities, including Ping-Pong tables and track-and-field. My Third Uncle's building next door to our house was rented to a couple of teachers, who operated a small private school. It had only two classrooms and a room for Ping-Pong. My cousin Suey Lung and I often sneaked into this building to play, as his mother had extra keys.

Kikbo is played by kicking a shuttlecock, made with the feathers of a rooster or pheasant, up in the air, without allowing it to fall to the ground. I was learning to kick with the inside of my right foot, and I could play kikbo by myself by counting the number of times I could keep it in the air, or kick it back and forth with other boys.

By Grade 4, I could read well enough to spend many hours over Chinese novels. *Romance of the Three Kingdoms* and *Westward Travels* were my favourite Chinese classics. On weekends or on holidays, I loved to rent comic books for a fraction of the cost of purchasing them. Most vendors displayed their goods on the sidewalks of busy streets, and often I could be found sitting on a stool reading, mostly kung-fu and historical stories. Only two or three times a year was I allowed to go to a movie; I saw Laurel and Hardy, a couple of John Wayne cowboy films, and Tarzan.

While these recreational activities may appear dull and unimaginative to the younger generation, still, we had fun, and I especially appreciated the relatively peaceful years after the war. My mother and I certainly were much happier and hopeful. We looked forward to many years of my attending Pui Ching Junior and Secondary schools, with the possibility of going abroad to Canada or the United States for university. Little did we know that we would soon be engulfed in the horrors of another war: Mao Zedong's Communists fighting against Chiang Kai-shek's Nationalists.

9

THE EAST IS RED

Civil war had heated up soon after Japan surrendered in 1945. How had Communism conquered China and was Ho Gor really a Communist? I had asked my mother these questions. She told me that she had some doubts about whether my cousin was really a member of the Communist Party, although he did work for the Communists, because he could read and write, while most of the Communists in Xin Hui were illiterate peasants. It might have been a way to avoid starvation, because the Communists in their revolutionary days had the reputation of believing in sharing, while too many Nationalists paid only lip service to democracy, and were more interested in political power and personal wealth than fair dealings with the general population. I believed that was why Communism swept through the land like a wildfire, starting in the northeast of China immediately after the war ended. However, almost immediately Generalissimo Chiang's Guomindang, known as the Nationalists, started fighting viciously for advantage against the Communists of Mao Zedong. Each was grabbing for land, cities, and industrial centres vacated by the

Japanese. Winds of war again whipped up from Manchuria, but this time Chinese were fighting Chinese!

Our city Canton was in the province of Guangdong in the south of China, far away from the conflicts in the northeast, but we heard the news and were extremely worried that the civil war was spreading out of control. The battles heated up on several fronts, and tens of thousands, including civilians, were killed. Refugees fled southward.

At the beginning, the Nationalists appeared to be much more powerful, because they were in control of the major cities and the country's financial and industrial centres. They also enjoyed the unequivocal support of the United States, because Americans generally trusted those Chinese who were Christians or had visited America. In particular, they favoured the ones who had gone to American schools, such as Madame Chiang Kai-shek, Mayling Soong, a Methodist and a graduate of Wellesley College. Her brother, T.V. Soong, a graduate of Harvard, became the minister of finance for Chiang. At the same time, America had a deep mistrust of the Communists, and refused to provide any aid to Mao, who then turned to Russia for help. Both Presidents Roosevelt and Truman provided military hardware, training, and financial aid to Chiang. However, many people, including Winston Churchill, had considered Chiang Kai-shek and his government inept and corrupt. He made serious mistakes in the man-agement of his armed forces and monetary policies. Many Nationalists, the intelligentsia, and even a couple of regional warlords were idealistic and patriotic individuals, who had good intentions and worked hard to bring democracy and justice to the common people, for a New China. Unfortunately, they were not powerful enough to exert any major influence on Chiang's central government.

Inflation was rampant; it ruined many ordinary citizens and affected our daily lives. Mother bought me a new pair of leather shoes at the beginning of the school year. Six months later I got a larger pair of shoes, identical to the first, but the price had jumped more than a hundred times! The value of newly issued currencies plummeted within a few months of their issue. My parents owned two rental buildings in the city. When I went with Mother to collect rents from our properties, we had to insist upon American dollars or gold bars as currency.

Occasionally we got some news from the free press in Hong Kong that the Communists were winning, particularly the hearts and minds of the masses, with their ideology and discipline, while the Nationalists were losing people's confidence by their ineptness and rampant corruption. Some of their generals and officials were embezzling funds from the Nationalist government and from private citizens. Our city newspapers reported glowingly Chiang's every little success and downplayed his mistakes. The Communists were depicted as horrific murderers and plunderers of people's wealth; the press was tightly controlled. However, we were able to gain some insight into the reality of things by talking to our visitors from Hong Kong, such as my cousin Che King. He spoke enthusiastically about Mao Zedong and Chou En-lai. He said that the Communists were united, disciplined, and gaining the support of most people, particularly the poor farmers, to whom they had promised small plots of land when the holdings of the rich landowners were liquidated. In the battlefields, Mao's soldiers, with far inferior weapons and no air force, defeated Chiang's larger armies, because too many of the Nationalist soldiers lacked motivation and often surrendered en masse. Their American-made weapons fell into the hands of the Communists.

One day in 1947, I was walking home from school when I saw soldiers chasing a man down the street. He brushed past me and nearly knocked me down, then jumped into the nearby Pearl River. Bang! Bang! Shots rang out. I sneaked through the crowd to the riverside and saw a body floating face-down in the water, a patch of red around him. They said he was a Communist.

The Nationalists were retreating in panic. Hordes of soldiers, college students, and refugees poured into our city, hoping that there was time enough to escape to Taiwan. They slept wherever they could put down their bedding. Some forced their way into our courtyard and camped. We were frightened, because many of them were loud and unruly. A few openly urinated outside our door. When my mother complained to the police, they said they could do nothing. Mother said that the police were afraid to intervene, not wanting to risk their lives when they were paid so miserably. Chaos, official corruption, and lawlessness ruled.

The Red Army crossed the Yangtze River and advanced towards our city virtually unopposed. Chiang's capital of Nanjing fell in April 1949, followed by Shanghai a month later. Our city was panic-stricken, because newspapers reported on the horrors that the Communists were committing: confiscating all personal property, exiling people to labour camps, and executing many political prisoners, landlords, capitalists, and bourgeoisie. While we did not own any farmland, nor had we oppressed any peasants, we did have those two rental buildings. Every night I heard gunfire in the streets, and more refugees poured into our city. A few times vicious fights erupted in front of my eyes. I was frightened walking outside, even during the day on my walk to school. I wanted desperately to leave China before it was too late. I wrote to my father and asked him if he could arrange visas for Mother and me to go to Canada. He wrote back on a blue aerogram, saying that he could not, because Canadian laws would not permit us to enter the country. I was sullen and frustrated. Why, then, did he marry my mother and have me when he knew that Canadian laws would not recognize his second wife and son?

In the spring of 1949, Fourth Uncle was visiting us from Canada. He stayed in our home, because his wife, Sai Sum, was living with us. I asked him why my father had not come to see us when the war ended. Or returned with him this time? He was slow in answering me, but finally said that my father was very busy working, trying to save for retirement. I was extremely unhappy hearing that, since peace had come four years before; there had been plenty of time for my father to make the trip to see us, if he really wanted to. I felt that he simply did not love us enough. Except for one old photograph, I did not even know what he looked like!

With the arrival of summer in 1949, more and more gunfights erupted in our streets. Chiang Kai-shek and his Nationalists were losing badly to the Communists, and Chiang's soldiers were retreating south towards our city, Canton being his last stronghold in the mainland before he fled to the island of Taiwan. A fierce battle was looming.

Every night curfew was enforced and soldiers were everywhere on our streets, all carrying guns. The political atmosphere was very tense. Mother warned me not to wander outside without her permission and insisted on walking me to school.

When I started Grade 5 in September, many of my former classmates had not returned, and each day one or two more were missing. Teachers and students often asked each other: How close are the Reds? Are you planning to leave the city? Where will you go? We were talking the panic talk.

Fourth Uncle and Sai Sum, Third Aunt, and my mother gravely discussed what to do. Fourth Uncle agreed to help, and he wrote to my father. Around 1950, only unmarried sons and daughters of a naturalized Canadian citizen who were under the age of nineteen were qualified to apply for immigration to the country. Nephews and nieces or any person wanting to emigrate to Canada had to buy false identity papers and were called "paper sons" or "paper daughters." My father could not sponsor me, because his second wife (my mother) had no legal status in Canada. It was decided that I would pose as a "paper son" to my Third Uncle, obtaining an identity card as his son to get into Canada. My Third Uncle had only one wife, thus he could claim me as his son.

On October 1, 1949, my Fourth Uncle and I were in a bookstore listening to the news on the radio when Mao Zedong spoke. From the viewing stand atop the Tiananmen Gate in Beijing, he proclaimed that the People's Republic of China was founded, and a million people could be heard singing "The East Is Red."

Before dawn on the morning of October 3, after bribing some officials to get the train tickets, Fourth Uncle led the group of us on foot to the train station, heading to Hong Kong, where we would make applications for visas to Canada. Ten days later, on October 13, 1949, the Red Army captured our city.

10

FATHER'S SOJOURN IN GOLD MOUNTAIN

"Where is BaBa and why is he not with us?" I had asked my mother more than once when growing up. I didn't remember ever seeing him around. She told me that my father was in Gum Saan, meaning Gold Mountain, a name the Chinese gave to North America because of the gold rushes of the previous century. She said that I should ask Fourth Uncle, because he knew my father best, and was much more learned than she. Over several evenings, I listened to my uncle's stories in the summer of 1949.

BaBa had gone to Canada to work and send remittances to support Grandma and the whole family living in Nam Bin. He had left his village and country in 1912, at a time when China was in political and economic chaos, suffering from civil wars and foreign imperialism.

Beginning in the nineteenth century and continuing into the first half of the twentieth, Western powers such as Great Britain used superior military might to force-sell opium and other goods to the Chinese. The

United States of America, Japan, and other European countries also forced an Open Door policy on the country. This meant foreign powers had opportunities for commerce in Chinese territory, with little or no control by the Chinese government. The once rich and proud Chinese Empire was being partitioned and impoverished, reduced in status like a semi-colony. Russia seized Mongolia, Japan controlled Manchuria, and Britain had Hong Kong.[1]

The Qing Dynasty was ready to collapse. The Republicans, led by Dr. Sun Yat-sen, were pressuring the Manchu emperor to abdicate, while trying to set up a democratic republic. Confusion and disunity ruled. Unemployment was rampant. Like many poor Cantonese of his generation, my father had to go abroad for work and the opportunity to make a living, and also support the family back home. He had intended the journey to be a sojourn, perhaps for thirty to forty years, and then he would return to his homeland for his golden years. He hoped his nation would then be a peaceful, democratic republic. That was the motivation for all those old-timers, but did it work out that way?

Historically, the Chinese had travelled far and wide around the globe for thousands of years. They rode along the Silk Road to Persia and Europe; they sailed to Java, Japan, and the Philippines. Some historians write that the Chinese explored America half a century before Columbus. From the middle of the nineteenth century, the young men from the southern Province of Guangdong were particularly attracted to North America, first as gold prospectors and later as labourers to build the transcontinental railways in the United States and Canada. After the railroads were built, they came to work in service industries like laundries or restaurants, to earn an honest living in any way possible.

In the nineteenth and early twentieth century, China suffered horribly from a series of political, economic, and natural disasters: The Opium War (1839–42), the Taiping Rebellion of peasants (1850–64), the first war against Japan (1894–95), and the Boxer Rebellion against foreigners (1898–1901). When exacerbated by the extravagance, incompetence, and corruption of the Manchu rulers, this inevitably led to the downfall of the Qing – or Manchu – Dynasty, and the establishment of the Republic of China in 1912. However, the country was very unstable, with feeble central control of the warring factions.

Regional warlords and bandits ruled the country. A rapidly growing population and natural disasters fostered ever more chaos, famine, and poverty. These harsh conditions forced some men into becoming bandits, who robbed and kidnapped. If ransoms were not paid, a severed hand or head might show up in the victim's home. Young men of good character like my father wanted to get out of such a terrible environment. They wanted to earn a living honourably, even if they had to leave their homeland, to work an ocean away among mainly unfriendly people with strange looks, languages, cultures, and restrictive laws. Chinese were generally not welcome in the host countries, due to prejudice. The hardships were unimaginable for those pioneers, especially not knowing the language and enduring bitter cold and long winters. They were a stoic lot.

My father and my uncles had to travel to Canada to earn a living because his father's addiction to opium had depleted the family's fortune. Grandfather Yuk Goh loved to lie around to smoke and dream, not wanting to do much of anything. Gradually he became a hermit and neglected to work the land that he had inherited from my great-grandfather Gim Sing. Good farmland was sold piece by piece to support his debilitating habit, so that, by the beginning of the twentieth century, the growing family was severely impoverished and desperately needed employment to survive. This was very difficult at the time, as civil war was still raging and warlords were fighting each other.

In his mid-teens, my father began to search for opportunities. His older brother, Su Dat, had gone to California early in the 1890s, working

in farming, but he was not very successful, partly because of racial discrimination. He returned to China very discouraged, and advised his younger
siblings not to go to America. However, my father knew a distant cousin,
Wah Bing, who had worked in Toronto and owned a hand laundry. He had
returned to his home village with a tidy fortune, enough to build a new
luxury home and buy some land. This villager's son, Buck Yet, and my father
were good friends, and they planned to immigrate to Canada. BaBa borrowed
money from his older married sister and the local benevolent association to
pay for his ship passage and the Government of Canada's exorbitant $500
head tax, a measure designed exclusively to discourage Chinese from coming
to Canada. This was a policy of systematic discrimination; immigrants from
Europe were not treated the same way, and were welcomed with open arms.
In 1912, my father left his mother and young bride, Lee Hees, to travel by
ship to Vancouver and then by train to Toronto.

At twenty-one, with a young wife and an elderly mother to support back
in the village, he found work in a grocery store in Toronto's Chinatown.
Within two years, he had saved enough to go into a business on his own,
by purchasing a laundry on Logan Avenue (it later moved to 908 Kingston
Road), becoming one of a majority of Canada's Chinese immigrants in the
laundry business. In his book *Enduring Hardship: The Chinese Laundry in
Canada*, Bang Seng Hoe reported that, by 1941, there were 6,143 Chinese
in Ontario, and a vast majority of them worked in laundries.

In 1919, he had heard that the Canadian government was considering
enacting The Chinese Exclusion Act, which would bar nearly all Chinese
from entering Canada. This law was similar to the one that had been
passed by the American Congress in 1882, which effectively halted Chinese
immigration to the United States. My father was anxious to be reunited
with Lee Hees before it was too late. Thus, in 1920, he had saved enough to
pay another $500 head tax and the sea passage to bring his wife to Canada.
In 1923, the federal government passed legislation which totally excluded

Chinese immigration, except for a few diplomats, students, and merchants. This Exclusion Act lasted for twenty-four years, and was finally repealed after the Second World War, in 1947, after vigorous appeals to the federal government by Chinese Canadians.

My stepmother, whom I called Dai Ma, was a small woman, but sturdy and hard-working. She gave birth to a son, Howard, in 1922 and a daughter, Dorothy, in 1923. When these two were old enough to help, they ironed shirts on padded wooden tables and served customers after school. The laundry work was physically demanding and the hours long, very often from early morning to late at night, six days a week, with little time for meals and leisure. Dai Ma and some hired help did most of the manual work, while Father drove a vehicle for pickups, deliveries, and the recruiting of new customers. Father, Dai Ma, and my older brother and sister all had an indomitable spirit and a capacity for hard work, and created an inspiring example for me to do my utmost to succeed.

My grandfather had been able to afford only a few years of formal schooling for my father and his three brothers, but not his sisters. Father had an exceptional ambition for his own children to go to university, whatever the cost in tuition and the time away from helping at the laundry. Higher education was out of reach at the time for most of the immigrant children, mainly because of racism and the high cost. In the first half of the twentieth century, a majority of second-generation Chinese Canadians did not go beyond middle or high school; they most often became tradesmen, secretaries, or small businessmen. Streaming of students by educators from junior schools to trade or occupational schools was common practice. However, my older siblings defied the odds and did manage to attend the University of Toronto. Howard would graduate in Electrical Engineering and Dorothy in Finance and Commerce. They were among the earliest Chinese youth in North America to obtain degrees, and served as role models to us younger folks. Recently, Howard published a book on our family history and the

Chinese in North America called *Golden Opportunities: The Contribution and Developments of the Chinese in Early North America*. He inspired me to write this memoir.

My father made a trip to China in 1928, with several purposes in mind. One was to see his mother and to celebrate her seventy-fifth birthday, an important filial duty he highly valued. Another reason was to bring his Canadian-born children home to meet their grandmother, and for some Chinese schooling. The third reason was to find a second wife.

In my father's time, and in traditional Chinese society, it was fashionable for a prosperous man to have more than one wife. His intention was to find a capable woman to take care of his aged mother, young enough to bear him more children, and trustworthy enough to manage his assets in China. This is when he built our new three-storey, Western-style house in Canton, and later bought a five-storey commercial building in Canton's business district. He believed that one day his entire family: First Wife, Second Wife, and all his children could live in a peaceful and prosperous China, enjoying the good life. He had expected to retire someday to his native land, after a sojourn of about thirty-five years in Gum Saan. This was his hope.

When he was in Canton, he gave an elaborate birthday party to honour his mother, with many relatives and friends coming from afar. He found land, hired an architect, and built his modern house at 12 Guan Yick Road in the fashionable residential East Hill district of the city. At the same time, my father helped to finance and supervise the construction of two buildings right next door for his younger brothers (my Third and Fourth uncles). A bridge was constructed, joining our building to that of my uncles at the third-floor level, so that my grandmother, who had bound feet, could move freely from one home to the other without having to climb stairs.

Upon the recommendation of his eldest sister, whom I called Dai Qhoo, he found an able-bodied twenty-year-old young woman living in his sister's village. Thus, in the summer of 1929, he married my mother, Lee

Yet Knor (aka Liat Knor Lee). My mother gave him a son, born in 1930, who unfortunately died from a childhood illness when he was two years old. This tragedy devastated my mother, particularly because my father was not there to share her grief. He was back in Toronto by then. Whenever I asked her about this deceased brother, she refused to tell me any details. Her face turned grave, as if she were still in pain.

Fortunately, my father made another trip to China in 1936, and I was born a year later. My grandmother was gone by then, but she did live for a while in the new house, with my mother being one of the caregivers. My mother was so grateful to be given a son that on numerous occasions she took me with her to Buddhist temples, to kneel and bow to Guan Yin, the Goddess of Mercy and Fertility. She would light some incense sticks for me to put into urns in front of the gently smiling goddess.

In later years, I also learned much about my father from Cousin Joe Jen, who in his youth lived for several years with my father and Dai Ma in Toronto. I visited his house on Bedford Road frequently, as it was located close to the University of Toronto. Very often, I was invited to dinner, and I always felt welcome, even when I dropped in unannounced. We talked well into many evenings, and I learned a lot about my father.

He told me that Father was well-respected both in China and Canada. Foremost, he was a good person, honest and hard-working. He helped to bring many relatives to Canada, such as his two younger brothers and two nephews, constantly giving them guidance and financial help. Relatives and friends often stayed for weeks or months in his home while they were getting settled or while job-hunting. All our friends and relatives spoke highly of Father and Dai Ma. He was active in the Chinese community, raising funds for charities and the Chinese war efforts during the Second World War. He served as president of the Kuo Min Tong Association in Ontario, a patriotic Nationalist organization working for democracy and peace in China.

It was difficult for me to judge him because I would know him for less than two years, at a time when he was not at his best, and in pain, but I never heard anyone say anything unfavourable about him. As a son, I am thankful for his good genes and I should focus on his good qualities and intentions.

11

ACROSS THE PACIFIC TO CANADA

The ship was waiting. Anxiety and sadness gripped me as I trudged up the gangway to board the big ocean liner. I was happy to leave war-torn China, and to follow in my father's footsteps to North America. After a separation of twelve years, I was nervous about meeting Father and his first wife and family. At the same time, I dreaded leaving my mother behind. She would be very lonely, since we had never been apart. How long would it be before we would meet again? Only God knew! She would be going back to Canton to live in Communist China, a nation in turmoil and isolation, still fighting viciously with Chiang Kai-shek. All kinds of conflicting emotions welled up in me.

How I wished that my mother was going with me, but she didn't have a passport. I had obtained a bogus passport as my uncle's "paper son." I was perplexed at our family situation and Canadian regulations.

We had had to pass a very intense interrogation at the Canadian consulate in Hong Kong. I went through more than an hour of harrowing questions by a Chinese-speaking lady officer.

My cousin Suey Lung (Albert) and I, identified on paper as brothers, had been put in separate rooms at the consulate and asked many questions, such as what we had for dinner the previous day. We also had to give descriptions of our house and each occupant and the names and characteristics of our neighbours. The officer's objective was to find out if we were true brothers or to trip us up if we were not. If they had found any discrepancies in our answers, they would have concluded that we had lied about our identities and relationships and would have denied our applications.

Numerous paper sons and daughters had gone to the United States and Canada, because people were desperate to get out of China when the Communists were conducting purges and tightening total control over everyone. Many young men paid around $2,000 each to buy a bogus paper. There were no guarantees of success, and many failed. However, I passed my interview, and the next hurdle was to undergo a very thorough physical examination by an immigration doctor, and submit to chest X-rays. Any signs of a previous or present lung infection, such as tuberculosis, would have caused a long delay for treatment or outright refusal of permission to enter Canada. I had had a lung infection when living in Xin Hui during the war, and was worried about the results, but I was lucky. I was diagnosed with having some scar tissue in the lining of my lungs, probably caused by pleurisy in childhood, but I was no longer infectious. The doctors gave me the green light.

It was December 24, 1949, when I walked towards the ship and read in block letters across its hull the words *General Gordon*. Fourth Uncle told me that it was a transport ship that had been used to carry American troops. It looked colossal to me compared to the Star Ferries crossing Victoria Harbour from Kowloon to Hong Kong Island. I was accompanied by Fourth Uncle, his two wives (one held false papers), and Cousin Suey Lung. A young man named Jow Gor came with us; he had bought a forged paper, also claiming to be a son of Fourth Uncle. I had heard that Jow Gor's father had paid Fourth Uncle some $1,500 Canadian for the false paper document. This practice was common at the time, the only way for many young people to obtain passports to enter Canada.

As the ship started moving and its horn shrieked, scattering the squawking seagulls in all directions, I stood on the second deck, with my body pressing against the rail. I thought I saw my mother still wiping her eyes. For several minutes, I continued to gaze ashore, hoping to keep her in sight for as long as possible, but her receding figure became blurry as a flood of silent tears clouded my focus. Bright lights and flashy neon signs blinked endlessly on Kowloon to the left of me and Hong Kong Island to the right, as our ship accelerated towards the open sea. I was heading to a strange land, to live with a family that I hardly knew.

The ship's crew and passengers were in a jolly mood, and the ship was decorated with Christmas lights and ornaments. I felt forlorn, and much of the time stayed in my bunk, in a large dormitory on a lower deck reserved for third-class passengers. The first night I slept fitfully and felt woozy as the ship tossed and lurched.

The next day was Christmas, and the cafeteria set out a huge array of food, all colourful but so strange-looking. The roasted chicken was so much bigger than the ones in our village; one slice of breast meat filled my entire dinner plate. I found out later that it was some monstrous bird called a turkey. It tasted rubbery and dry, even with the thick brown goo that my uncle called gravy. I ate only a couple of mouthfuls. The bread and rice puddings were tasty and served as my Christmas dinner, together with a glass of sweet tea mixed with condensed milk and an orange. How I missed my mother's steamed minced pork with salted fish and a bowl of white rice!

For two days, the sea was rough; my two aunts were seasick and threw up a few times. Since I felt better the next afternoon, I visited them and brought them tea. Two more days of sailing under a cloudy sky, and our ship arrived at Yokohama. We were happy that it had at last stopped moving, if only for a few hours. We breathed in the salty air and gazed at the dull old buildings, some still with gaping holes from American bombings. We stayed aboard, because this Japanese seaport looked desolate and poverty-stricken. I certainly had no desire to go ashore and see the people who had so recently inflicted such pain and suffering on my mother and me and millions of others.

After we left Japan, on December 29, the sea became calmer and the sun was warm and soothing. What a joy when we arrived in Hawaii on January 4, 1950. The hills looked so lush and the beaches so inviting. Unfortunately, we did not have any visas to visit the United States and had to watch from the deck. Colourful ladies in loose-fitting dresses and little girls in grass skirts were dancing, swaying and gesturing with their hands to the haunting music that was so distinctive of Hawaii. On the other side of the ship some passengers were throwing coins down into the ocean, and little boys were diving to catch them. I threw a couple of nickels that I had won from the slot machine, and the boys dived in after them. They surfaced soon afterwards and two boys flashed their catches to us, then stuffed the coins in their mouths and waved to us to toss more coins.

For the next few days we all felt better as the huge waves shrank to little whitecaps. On January 9, our ship glided under the famed Golden Gate Bridge to dock at the gold-rush city of San Francisco. After sixteen days at sea, we were very happy to be on solid ground, but without visas we were only allowed to walk into a customs building, and then into a guarded bus that took us directly to the train station, heading for Vancouver.

On the train, I searched hard to see any gold-paved streets or gold-painted buildings, but to my disappointment I saw only grey concrete everywhere, without a speck of the precious metal. As our train sped northward, the scenery turned brighter as I saw white powder falling and covering everything. Then the sun peeked through the thick clouds, and I had my first glimpse of a winter wonderland.

When we got off the train in Vancouver on January 12, snow was falling in feathery flakes. I tried to catch it with my hands and tongue. It was enchanting, but then I felt my toes cold and wet as I sloshed through the slushy mess outside the station, wearing only my black leather shoes. A taxi took us to Chinatown on Pender Street. The first thing our group wanted to do, after checking into a small hotel, was to go for Cantonese food. We went to a restaurant called Bamboo House. The steamed minced pork, rice, and congee had never tasted so good!

We had intended to rest in Vancouver for two or three days before taking the train to Toronto. However, an avalanche of snow had buried some tracks in the Rocky Mountains, so my Fourth Uncle decided to stay a week, to rest and visit some relatives, before setting out eastward on January 26.

The sight of the Rockies was awe-inspiring, with the grey mountains, capped by snow, rising thousands of feet into the sky. Our train looked tiny and insignificant as it chugged and twisted through valleys, canyons, and long, dark tunnels. I was frightened that an avalanche might bury us, or push us off the tracks to certain death.

Coming in the opposite direction were ploughs, clearing huge piles of drifts on the tracks. I was continually delighted and awed by the panoramic views unfolding every mile: tall snow-capped mountains, turquoise glacier lakes, majestic firs and pines. I told myself that someday, when I had money, I would take this train and visit these mountains again, preferably in summer or fall. Our smoke-belching iron machine climbed ponderously for a day and night before descending cautiously; then it picked up speed, and suddenly the grand mansion of Château Lake Louise appeared, draped in snow and bathed in brilliant sunshine.

My uncle told me the story of how thousands of Chinese labourers had helped to build the railroad, and many died from dynamite accidents, malnutrition, brutal winters, inadequate medical care, landslides, mudslides, snake bites, attacks from grizzly bears, and other tragedies. It was estimated that one Chinese died for each mile of track built. I was also told how badly the Chinese workers were treated. They had to do the harder and riskier tasks, such as blasting tunnels through huge rocks, and yet they were paid about half of what the white workers were paid. I became nervous as I listened, because I thought of the many ghosts that must be haunting these mountains; they might even try to derail our train to kill us and then steal our souls!

The next day we entered flat land – very flat land. I saw wide expanses of snow for miles and miles, covering wheat fields and cattle ranges. Villages were few and far apart. For about an hour I counted on average nearly two hundred telephone poles between houses. Rarely did I see people outside, but at a small town I saw several children chasing a little black ball with big sticks on a pond; sometimes they fell down, and they yelled with glee. I had no idea what they were playing.

Two days later our train pulled into Winnipeg, where we changed trains. While we waited on the platform for the Toronto train, I decided it must be the windiest and coldest place on earth. Even my long johns, two sweaters, a coat, and two pairs of woollen socks could not stop my shivering. I breathed clouds of smoke, and I was fearful that Toronto might be worse.

Finally, on January 31, five weeks after leaving my mother, we arrived at Union Station. In a huge hall, we met my father. Everyone seemed to talk at once. I was shy, because Father was a stranger to me; I had not seen him since I was an infant. I looked up at a tall and gaunt man, a faintly familiar figure from an old photograph. All I could say was "BaBa," as tears welled up in my eyes.

He gave my head a pat, "Ah Lun, are you warm enough? You must be hungry. Let's go home." That's all I remember of what he said or did. Thus, I began my new life in Gold Mountain.

12

TO KILL A CLUCKING BIRD

On the first Sunday after my arrival in Toronto, BaBa took me to visit Chinatown, just the two of us. He said that we were to have lunch, meet friends, and to buy a chicken for dinner. He drove a grey Dodge sedan from our house on Beaty Avenue, in Toronto's Parkdale, east along Queen Street for about twenty minutes. When we reached a wide boulevard, which he told me was called Dai Hawk Guy, "University Avenue," we stopped behind a red-and-white streetcar, as passengers got on and off. There was a divider in the middle of the road, and the traffic flowed up and down on both sides. I looked to my left and saw a tall, imposing building. BaBa told me this building housed the Canada Life Assurance Company. He pointed up to the beacon on the roof and explained that it was flashing a white light, which indicated snow. It was true. I looked at the little white flakes dancing across the sky and falling gently onto our windshield, instantly becoming wet spots. Father turned a handle to open the window and stuck his left hand out, as a blast of chilly air smacked my face. When I asked him why he stuck his hand out into the cold, he said that he was signalling a left turn.

After two or three minutes of driving up University Avenue, BaBa announced that we had arrived at the Chinese Presbyterian Church, near the corner of Dundas Street. He parked in front of the small building, and I followed him up several steps and entered a large room with about a dozen people. A short, dapper man named Mr. Mark approached us and gave a large brown envelope to my father. He said it contained some insurance policies. He then gave me a dollar bill as a Geen Mien Lai, a "first time meeting" gift.

We then walked to a side street, where we climbed to the second floor of a three-storey building. I saw a wooden sign on which was written Gee Duk Tong in Chinese. My father explained that this was a benevolent society for the men who bear the family names of Wu, Chow (spelled Joe in my case), Choi, Yung, and Tao. When we entered the room, several men shouted loudly, "Ney Ho Ma? How're you?" They were sitting around talking, sipping tea, smoking, or reading the *Sing Wah Bo*, a Chinese newspaper.

After about half an hour of loud conversations among the men, mostly in the Sze Yup dialect from my village, my father invited a man I called Uncle Siu Bah to come with us to Yum Char for dim sum and tea. The three of us walked a few minutes to reach a café called Cathay Garden on Elizabeth Street near Queen. I had a dai bow, which is a big bun filled with minced pork, Chinese sausage, and chicken. I also ate a har gow, which contained a big lump of minced pork and a bit of shrimp. For dessert, I shared with my father a sweet egg tart, which melted in my mouth. I found the Woo Lung tea too dark and strong, and so I asked for a cup of boiled water. This was a popular drink in China, because we often found that water from the tap was unsafe.

Uncle Siu Bah told me a little bit about Chinatown, since he had worked there at the Mon Kwok Trading Company for many years. He said that about two thousand Chinese lived in the area, with another thousand scattered throughout the city and the suburbs. Sunday was the busiest day in Chinatown, as the Chinese came to eat, socialize, visit herbal doctors, and shop, particularly for groceries. On leaving, he gave me a Lei-see, a small red envelope that contained lucky money. Inside I found a one-dollar bill.

After lunch, my father and I walked along Elizabeth Street and stopped at Siu Yuen Barbeque, where BaBa bought a slice of roasted pig. He introduced me to the owner, Uncle Yue Suk, and his wife, Yue Sum, who was the cashier, and she gave me a dollar. Our last stop was at a noisy and smelly poultry shop, where BaBa bought a live chicken from a Mr. Wasserman. The owner tied the bird's feet, wrapped it in newspapers with the head sticking out, and then put it in a big brown paper bag. I carried the bird to the car and sat next to it; several times its beak pecked furiously on my knee and it made a constant clucking noise.

I was bewildered by the names of all the folks that I had met that day, how they were related to me, and where in China they had come from. In the car, I consulted with my father and jotted down in my little notebook the people and events of the day.

Back in the kitchen of our home, I watched BaBa take a firm hold of the clucking bird, bend its head back, and, with a slash of the knife, cut the throat. Bright red fluid shot out in a long arc into the sink. He then soaked the chicken in hot water for several minutes, after which he plucked the feathers and cleaned out the innards. I helped by pulling out the last fine feathers with tweezers.

My father immersed the naked bird in water that was very hot, but not quite boiling. I was to watch the pot to make sure the chicken was cooked just right, which took nearly an hour. He then took it out and chilled it quickly under the cold-water tap to make the skin kind of crispy. BaBa explained that this was a traditional Chinese recipe. A mixture of salt, finely chopped green onion, and ginger were mixed with oil in a bowl, to serve as a dip for the chicken. He used the broth from the chicken as a stock for making a soup. I helped in picking out tiny feathers from a bowl containing pale-coloured flakes, which he said was a bird's nest that had also previously been soaked in water. He boiled this in the broth for half an hour, and then mixed in some finely diced Virginia ham. We made bird's-nest soup, a nourishing and rare delicacy I loved, even though a few very tiny bits of feather still floated in the liquid. As to the name Bird's Nest, it has been a favourite food for the Chinese since ancient times; the ingredient is the actual stored food in the nests of seabirds, like honey is the food of bees stored in their hives. I used to eat it frequently, but not in recent years, because it is too expensive – several hundred American dollars a pound.

That was a most scrumptious dinner, and I wished that my own mother had been there with me, to enjoy BaBa's fine cooking. Incidentally, that was the only time my father and I together bought a live chicken; after that, the chickens that we cooked came mostly from local grocery stores and were less tasty. My father never cooked much after that, because his health quickly deteriorated.

The chicken and the bird's-nest soup were the highlights of the best meal that I had ever enjoyed in my youth; I was also richer by three dollars. The day was most unforgettable, because BaBa and I had spent it together, a good beginning for us to get reacquainted. However, I had a premonition that there might not be many more such occasions for my father and me. I feared that we might be separated again.

13

I WISH I HAD SAID . . .

In 1951, my father's visits to doctors and hospitals increased dramatically, particularly those to the Mount Sinai Hospital on Yorkville Avenue. I listened quietly as my sister, brother, and Dai Ma discussed his illness and what to do. On one occasion, he and Dai Ma took the train to Windsor for three days to see a doctor specializing in his type of cancer. He came back looking tired and in obvious discomfort. In Toronto, when Dorothy was busy or Dai Ma was feeling unwell, I accompanied him several times for his visits to doctors, an acupuncturist, and a herbal shop in Chinatown. As summer passed into early autumn, I could see that his grey eyes were subdued by a cocktail of pills and 222s. His thin body was often curled up in bed or on the sofa, with sweating and chills. I covered him with a Hudson's Bay blanket, but he still felt cold. I helped my stepmother in caring for him. At first, I felt a little embarrassed handling his bedpans; I was alarmed when I noticed his urine was brownish, unlike mine, which looked very pale. I helped him bathe and dress. I sat on his bed to massage his back and comb his sparse hair before visitors came. About once a week, I took the streetcar to Chinatown to buy his favourite foods, particularly freshly butchered poultry from Mr. Wasserman, in the hope of boosting his appetite and minimizing his weight loss.

I regret that I did not get to know my father very well. In my naïveté, I had resented him for abandoning Mother and me during the war, and not returning to see us after it was over. He was in frail health when I reunited with him in 1950. Constantly visiting doctors and hospitals, he was not often in the mood to talk. We had so little quality time together. Because of his health, we hadn't done many of the father-son things that would have bonded us. I thought that my father was not particularly talkative or lovable, to my chagrin. I do not remember he ever really hugged me, or gave me a present, other than some Lei-sees, for New Year's and birthdays. I had wondered if other Chinese fathers were like that, or just mine. I was also shy, and initiated very few conversations with him.

I wish that I had learned things from him, like how to use an abacus, a fascinating instrument that I saw him using for adding, subtracting, and other calculations. On a couple of occasions, he read and explained to me stories from a famous historical novel, *The Three Kingdoms*. This classic was in an old edition, which he had read when he was a youth. I have kept this tattered book to this day, as one of my keepsakes. When he was dying, he did urge me again to study hard, not to work in a laundry if at all possible, and to bring my mother to Canada as soon as feasible. He said that he had not been able to do so because of Dai Ma's objections.

In October 1951, my family and I were visiting my father at Mount Sinai Hospital. As he lay there with tubes inserted into his nose and left arm, I watched his chest rise and fall, heaving occasionally. A nurse came in and put a thermometer in his mouth. He opened his eyes briefly, nodded his head, and closed his eyes again. On leaving, the nurse gave us a forced smile, and said, "Sorry, I think we have done all we can."

When my stepmother and my siblings went out for something to eat, I remained seated, chewing on a chocolate bar. The room was eerily quiet, except for the hissing of the respirator. I turned to look out the window, and reflected on my life with my father. I figured that the total time that we had together, including the three months when I was an infant, amounted to two years less a day. It was like a judge handling down a sentence on me.

Hearing a muffled cough, I got up and came closer to my father and asked in Cantonese, "BaBa, ney yu mut yeh? You want something?"

He opened his eyes, looked at me, and said, "Ah Lun, ney lay jor. Ho la! Alan, you have come. Good!"

I leaned forward to hear more, hoping that we could talk a bit, because I wanted to ask him some vital questions: Why hadn't he returned to China to see Mother and me?

He didn't say anything more and appeared to fall asleep again. Not having the heart to disturb his peace in what were perhaps his last days, I too remained quiet. Later, while riding in my brother's car on our way home, and listening to the grave conversation between Howard and Dorothy, I realized that we were about to lose our father. I believe that he had upheld a core set of values: basic human kindness, loyalty to family and friends, diligence, and community service. I wished I had said four more words to him. Something like, "BaBa, I love you."

Four days later, I stood solemnly at the side of a highly polished mahogany casket, looking at my father lying there on white silken fabric, looking peaceful, not as gaunt and pallid as when he was alive. The makeup artist had done a good job. He was wearing his favourite grey-flannel suit and a blue tie. One by one, friends and relatives came up to bow to him three times, then shook my hand or hugged me. I thanked them in a choking voice. A little later I watched an attendant in a black suit slowly close the lid. At fourteen, I felt he had abandoned me once more. With sadness and some bitterness in my heart, I realized that my mother's hope of seeing him again was forever dashed. I felt as if I had been robbed.

14

LIFE WITH DAI MA

Life with my stepmother had been uneasy at the beginning. It took several months for me to get more comfortable. The excitement of reuniting with my father after twelve years, and of seeing a new country, quickly wore off. I was soon overwhelmed with loneliness. I worried that my mother was all alone in Communist China, missing me as much as I was missing her. I found it difficult to relate to my new family: a stepmother and a half-sister and -brother who were fifteen and sixteen years older, respectively, than I. They were not really unkind to this boy who had suddenly been placed in their midst. Perhaps I was too sensitive, but I felt unloved. Dorothy was nice enough to sit with me one or two evenings a week, to teach me the English alphabet and pronunciations. Particularly, I had difficulty enunciating "r," as in rice, and "th," as in this.

Howard lived in St. Catharines, and I saw him only occasionally; at first, I was a little afraid of him. In traditional Chinese society, the first-born son is dominant, a father figure. I felt the most at ease with his wife, my sister-in-law, Hazel, who appeared the most friendly and caring. She always greeted me with a smile.

That first summer, I had a pleasant excursion to see the vast and lush countryside east of Toronto. Howard and Hazel took Dai Ma and me on a motor trip to the Kawartha area to see the lakes, the Trent Canal, and the locks that transport boats from one lake to another. We visited Peterborough and close family friend Henry Low, who entertained us in his Silver Moon Restaurant with delicious meals of T-bone steaks and local smallmouth bass, pickerel, or walleye. I had my first taste of the golden potato called a French fry and a dessert named Boston cream pie. Subsequently, I developed a craving for these North American foods. We stayed the night in a hotel in Peterborough, which our friend insisted on paying for. I enjoyed the trip very much and got to know Howard and Hazel a little better. Gradually, I became less afraid of my big brother.

Dai Ma was my father's first wife. I had felt awkward when I was instructed to call her Mama, or Dai Ma. I had called my biological mother Dai Jie, meaning Big Sister, since I learned to talk, and when I asked why I had to call her Dai Jie, while my friends called their mothers Mama, she explained that, according to Chinese custom, the first wife of a man is the official mother to all his children, and they must address her as Mother. I found that tradition disconcerting, particularly when I had to introduce a grey-haired woman as my MaMa to my school friends. I loathed explaining, because I felt the Canadian kids would never understand.

Dai Ma was nearly sixty years old when I first met her. She stood less than five feet tall, was a little stout, and looked weary. Age certainly had caught up to her, perhaps because she had spent decades working hard in my father's laundry business, raising two children, and caring for my father and many of his relatives. She had suffered some minor strokes, and often in church I had to nudge her when she started snoring. She was a devout Christian, and she did her best to feed and clothe me. I imagined it was probably a burden for her to have to raise a stepson in her retirement years, which should have been peaceful. Although she never yelled or punished me, still, I couldn't stop worrying about whether I was wanted or not. I avoided talking back to her, trying hard not to give her – or anyone – a reason to throw me out, particularly after my father's passing.

Our house at 85 Beaty Avenue was a three storey, semi-detached, red-brick house with a good-sized wooden porch, where I often sat and read. An majestic old chestnut tree stood on the front lawn; it gave me the pleasure of shade in summer and horse chestnuts to play with in autumn. We lived on the main floor, which had three bedrooms, and we rented out the rest as a rooming house. Before his death, my father had occupied the large front bedroom with big bay windows. My sister had the middle room, and Dai Ma had the smallest, measuring about seven-by-eleven feet, located next to the kitchen, with a window facing the backyard. I had begun my new life in this little room, taking up one third of Dai Ma's space. A narrow two-and-a-half-foot folding cot was placed at the other end of her room. I slept in that small alcove for nearly two years. A used walnut chest with three drawers, a small grey metal desk, and a steel folding chair with a thin red cushion filled up the rest of the space. It had taken me several weeks to get used to sharing a room with someone other than my own mother, and Dai Ma's snoring bothered me a little at the beginning.

A week after my arrival, Dai Ma had taken me by streetcar to Eaton's and Simpson's department stores to look for a warmer winter coat. These downtown stores, with five or six stories each, seemed huge. It looked as if they had everything for sale, even a boat? At Eaton's Annex, she chose a navy parka from the SALE rack. It hung loosely on me, but Dai Ma said it was large, "So that you can grow into it." When we got home, she folded the extra-long sleeves inward about one and a half inches and sewed them up by hand. The following December, she let the sleeves out, and I could see the frayed crease. Though not stylish, that parka did keep me warm enough my first two winters in Canada, and I never had a cold or the flu. However, I promised myself that someday I would have money, and I would walk into Eaton's or Simpson's to buy something that I really fancied.

Hard-working and thrifty, Dai Ma spent very little on cosmetics or jewellery for herself, but she had a sense of style. Her dresses, hats, and fur coat looked fashionable – more so than the clothes of many other Chinese aunties of her age that I encountered. She was frugal, and when she had taken me to the Queen Street Barbershop for my first haircut, she twice told the barber, "Cut short, short." I kept protesting, "No Short, No Short." When I came home to look in the mirror, I winced at how short my hair was and the unseemly sight of two dime-sized scars just above my right ear, where two boils had erupted one hot summer when I was a child. Before I went with Dai Ma to church that Sunday, I used a soft lead pencil to darken my pale bald scars. I wanted to look good, because several girls were usually there with their parents. The vanity of youth!

One day, the screen window to Dai Ma's bedroom had a large hole cut through it and her purse was stolen. The police were called but the thief was never caught. One afternoon, I came in from the backyard through the side door, and overheard Dai Ma talking on the phone about the burglary. She said, "I suspected that Alan might have done it." I was shocked, but I dared not confront her or tell my father about my innocence. I retreated to the backyard and quietly wept. I started to mow the lawn to deaden the hurt.

After my father's death, I continued to live quietly with Dai Ma and Dorothy, and took over more of the rooming-house chores and cooking, as Dai Ma's health was also deteriorating. In 1954, Dorothy married a very kind gentleman from Vancouver, Edward Yip. They lived for a year and a half in an apartment a few blocks from us, but when Dai Ma suffered another stroke, they moved back to our house and occupied the large front room, which I had moved into after my father's death. I, in turn, took my sister's old room, which was much darker and smaller, as it had only one window facing the neighbour's brick wall, about three and a half feet away. On hot summer nights, I had to keep the windows open, and sometimes was awakened by streetcars clanking along the rails on Queen Street.

15

MY FIRST MENTOR

Meeting an influential mentor early in my life in Canada was a defining moment. My destiny as a young immigrant was very much in doubt, but fortunately I encountered Mr. Perkins. He was the principal of the first school that I attended in Toronto, Fern Avenue Public School. After arriving in the middle of a bitter winter, I spent the first two months getting acquainted with my new surroundings, learning some English, and waiting for warmer weather. When the tulips began to raise their heads through the dark earth in our yard, I was ready and eager for school.

Hazel, my brother's wife, took me to the school that she had attended herself. She still remembered Mr. Perkins. Hazel and Dorothy talked about choosing an English name for me for school. They thought Alan might be good, since it sounded very close to my Chinese vernacular name, Ah Lun. I repeated two or three times, "Alan Joe, Alan Joe." I had to remember that, in the West, people put their family names last, instead of first like we Chinese do.

Strange practice, I thought.

At Fern Avenue Public School, we met a big stout man with greyish hair, who came forward from behind his desk to shake my hand, and he laughed heartily at whatever Hazel was saying to him. I recited to him my rehearsed speech, which I had learned from Dorothy: "Sir, my name is Alan Joe. And I thank you for accepting me to your very good school." I could not understand much of the remainder of the conversation, nor could I answer several questions that he asked me, except for how old I was and where I lived? Then I heard him say, "Grade 2."

I was disappointed, because I had been in Grade 5 in China. I felt humiliated to be put in with the little kids, who probably couldn't even wipe their own noses. I asked Hazel in Chinese to ask Mr. Perkins if he could put me in Grade 4. Hazel interpreted and told me he had said maybe he could do so in six months' or a year's time, when my English improved. He smiled and said something to me; he then made a phone call.

A few minutes later a blond-haired boy came into the office. Mr. Perkins introduced us and we shook hands. I learned that his name was Francis, and he escorted me to the classroom of Miss McKay, a large, matronly lady with wavy grey hair. She greeted me warmly and led me to a seat towards the back of the room. She gave me an exercise book and a pen with a pen nib and filled my inkwell with black ink. She instructed me with gestures to practise penmanship like the other boys and girls, by writing each letter of the alphabet several times. Later that morning Mr. Perkins visited our classroom and talked to the class about me and gestured to me to stand up. I didn't understand what he said, and sat stiffly at my cramped desk, but the class clapped their hands loudly. I saw many smiling faces. I didn't have any difficulty doing the arithmetic, but I couldn't sing the high notes of a song – which I learned later was called "The Maple Leaf Forever" – because my voice was changing, while my classmates still had high-pitched voices.

The next morning, upon my arrival, I found that a large, new desk had been installed in place of my small one. I could sit and write comfortably. At recess Mr. Perkins came over to greet me, and he brought with him a Chinese boy named David Mar from a higher grade. David was truly a big brother, and he helped me enormously in adjusting to my first year at the school, especially with improving my English. He had come to Canada a year before me, and he was also a bit older and wiser. We two were the only boys at the school who had come from China, while the other half-dozen or so Chinese children were Canadian-born and spoke very little Chinese. Most of them avoided us, looking at us as if we were country bumpkins!

By September of 1950, I was in Miss Murray's Grade 3 class. She was a young lady with a face full of freckles, rusty red hair, and dimples. She smiled a lot, and I liked her instantly. She paid special attention to me and stayed after class several times to help me with my grammar. I loved her and was a bit sad when Mr. Perkins told me before the Christmas holidays that I was to leave Miss Murray's class and to report to Miss Laurence's Grade 5 class in January 1951. My new teacher was a slim, tall lady who was quiet but friendly enough. I stayed half a year with Miss Laurence, and then Mr. Perkins advanced me to Grade 7, this time with a male teacher for a change.

Mr. Palmer was a handsome young man with a shallow cleft in his chin and a deep baritone voice. He was fun, laughed and hummed a lot, and talked to us about opera, playing us records of tenors Mario Lanza and Enrico Caruso. He said when he was a boy he used to listen to opera with his father and had wanted to be an opera singer, but I was glad he stuck to teaching. He was my favourite teacher at Fern Avenue Public School. One day in class he asked each of us what our parents did for a living and what we wanted to be. Many of the students seemed to wish to be like their parents, like a travel agent, policeman, or shopkeeper. A pretty girl of Chinese heritage named Angela said proudly that her father was a dentist and that she might want to be one too. I looked shyly at this tall, slim girl, and, when it was my turn, I said that I wanted to be a dentist. I also told the class that my father was ill and was not working. I was too embarrassed to say that my father was a laundryman, because the stereotypical Chinese portrayed in the North American media was often the lowly labourer, coolie, or houseboy. I was immature and vain.

I heard racial slurs frequently at school. I remembered a fight I had with a boy at the beginning of the school year when I entered Grade 7. Roy had taunted me, "Chinky chinky Chinaman. Washee washee my laundry." I was sensitive to the knowledge that my father occupied a particular stratum of Canadian society that was near the bottom of the totem pole, even though he had worked hard all his life, owned his own business, was a success in raising a fine family with two university graduates, and was a credit to his race and community – indeed, a good citizen Canada could be proud of. That day I vowed to study hard, to make my parents proud of me, and that my children would never be embarrassed to tell people what their father did for a living. Unlike most Chinese of my father's generation, I had so much more opportunity, because conditions had improved greatly in my time. I had no control over where I came from, or who my parents were, but where I was going depended entirely on me.

A proud event for me in Mr. Palmer's class was being elected president by my classmates, even though my English was still very poor. Another honour came to me when Mr. Perkins appointed me to be an official bell ringer, someone who pulled the bell for class to begin and end and for recess. He would often come to talk to me at recess time and ask about my studies and about my home life, particularly after he found out that my father had died in the fall of 1951 and that my own mother was still in Communist China. He gave me a pleasant surprise a week before Christmas of 1951, when he told me that I was to be promoted to Grade 8 with Miss Mutton in the New Year.

I found my new teacher was an aloof older woman, with grey hair and a stern countenance. Inserted halfway through the year, I felt lost much of the time and became frustrated. Luckily a boy named Steven befriended me and helped me with the lessons. I was seated at the very back of the classroom, and was seldom picked to answer any questions, for which I was glad. Somehow, I muddled through.

By the spring of 1952, I had been at Fern Avenue Public School for two years and three months, and it was time to apply to a secondary school. My friend Steven was going to Western Technical School, and he urged me to go with him. I was debating whether to become an electrician like Steven, or – if I really dared to dream – a dentist like Dr. Fred Pon, who was at that time, to my knowledge, the only Chinese dentist practising in Toronto. I was feeling very insecure after my father's death, because I did not know how soon I would have to go to work to support myself. I also wanted to bring my mother to Canada as soon as possible, because the civil war in China continued, and the Korean War was raging.

At that time, it was common practice for public-school educators to stream their Grade 8 students to Advanced or General high schools. So-called bright students, with good potential for university, were streamed to advanced-level schools, while the less academic and the children of immigrants, who were seen as having fewer prospects, were streamed to schools to learn a trade. I didn't know to which level I belonged.

I talked to Mr. Perkins about what high school I should attend, technical, commercial, or collegiate? He asked me to do an aptitude test and an IQ test. The following week he told me the result: I scored high in biology, creativity, and social sciences, but low in business. My IQ score was a little over one hundred, which was very average. When he saw how disappointed I looked, he explained that my English was still not too proficient, and that I probably had difficulties understanding the tests, particularly for the first time. He went on to say that he had had a couple of seemingly very ordinary students in the past, one of which went on to become a doctor and the other a lawyer and provincial court judge. He urged me to attend a school with a good arts-and-science program. His advice to me when I got up to leave was something like, "You don't have to be the brightest in the class; just smart enough will do. Hard work and determination are what you'll need. I have full confidence in you."

Taking his advice, I enrolled at Parkdale Collegiate Institute. I dared to dream that someday I would be some kind of a doctor, in dentistry or medicine. My high-school years went by rather quickly and were uneventful; I studied hard and worked on weekends, without much time for extracurricular activities. Most years I managed to rank second or third in my class of about twenty-five students, although, to my chagrin, I was never able to beat a dark-haired Ukrainian girl, who later became a well-known physician.

I visited Mr. Perkins once in a while when I was in Grades 9 and 10, but later lost touch with him when he retired. Then, some ten years later, on a Sunday afternoon when I was the dental resident on call at the Hospital for Sick Children, I got a surprise telephone call from Mr. Perkins. Apparently, he had gone to a matinee at the Royal Alexander Theatre and met an old acquaintance, Dr. Sandy MacGregor, a professor of mine. He learned that I was on duty at the hospital and called me. The following week we met at the hospital cafeteria for coffee; I was very happy to see him and expressed to him my heartfelt appreciation.

He was a mentor for me at a critical time when I was literally "fresh off the boat," and directed me on the path to a successful career and life. He challenged me to dare to dream and gave me the confidence to pursue an academic and professional career. I would have other mentors in later years, but he was the first. My conversation with Mr. Perkins when I was in Grade 8 was a defining moment in my life.

16

A $2 BILL

My first job earned me twelve dollars. My boss, Mr. Deng, handed me a ten-dollar and a two-dollar bill at the end of my first week working as a waiter at the High Park Grill. I tucked the cash into an inside pocket of my jacket, and my right hand kept touching the two bills as I walked home that evening in the early summer of 1952. That was my salary from my first paying job at the age of fourteen. It introduced me to North American cuisine, and it also gave me a tiny taste of financial independence, a sense of some control of my life. While my basic needs like food and shelter were provided by Dai Ma after my father's passing, I hated asking for money. I felt that I needed to find a summer job and earn my own pocket money. I didn't have much in the bank except the few dollars that I had saved from Lei-sees given to me at New Year's and birthdays. I decided that I must learn to work, because I felt unsure about everything. I wanted to buy my own things, such as books and supplies for high school, which were not provided free. I also wanted to buy myself a new coat for the coming winter, because the one that I had worn for two winters was frayed at the elbows, and I wasn't particularly fond of it.

To scout which stores might be hiring, I went walking around my neighbourhood one Friday after school. I discovered that there were several Chinese restaurants and grocery stores nearby on Queen and King streets. The following morning, I went to three restaurants and two fruit stores searching for a job. My English was not good, and I was afraid to go into English places, so I looked only into Chinese establishments. I was tired and disappointed at the end of that first day, but the owners were friendly and many loved talking to me in the dialects of Toi San or Xin Hui. I could also speak the dialect of Hong Kong. The next day, I walked an extra two to three miles to go further north on Roncesvalles Avenue. On Sundays, most businesses, except eating places, were closed because of city bylaws. I looked into two more coffee shops, but they were not hiring any summer help, because their own children would be helping.

Near Dundas Street, I looked through the window of the High Park Grill. A man in a rumpled white shirt with rolled-up sleeves and a stained half-apron wrapped around his waist was sitting at the Formica lunch counter drinking coffee or tea. I went in to introduce myself. He said he was the cook, called Loh Wong. The boss, Loh Deng, was away on an errand. He invited me to sit down on a circular green vinyl stool next to him and offered me coffee or a soft drink; I chose a Coca-Cola. He was eager to talk to me in his native tongue of Xin Hui, one of the Sze Yup County dialects common with the Chinese immigrants in Canada. Later, he invited me into the kitchen to keep him company while I waited for his boss. As I watched him peeling potatoes, I picked up a peeler to help him. I peeled some carrots, too, until the owner returned.

The cook introduced me to Mr. Deng, who was dressed neatly, in a starched white shirt and navy-blue trousers. He too spoke to me in his Xin Hui dialect and was delighted that I understood him. He invited me to sit with him at a table opposite the lunch counter, and asked a young waitress to bring me another Coca-Cola from the fountain. We talked about our ancestral villages and my family situation for several minutes. Then he asked me to wait while he went to finish planning the next day's menu. I watched him tapping on his typewriter with his two middle fingers. He then showed me the menu and asked me to read the first few items. I did my best, although I didn't know many of the words; most of the menu sounded foreign to me. He explained corned beef and cabbage to me, and mentioned that the menu changed each day: fish and chips was popular on Fridays and pot roast on Sundays. Then he gave me a blue carbon copy of the menu to study at home and said to report back to him in a week's time when school ended. The pay was two dollars per day for ten hours a day, six days a week, with Mondays off.

When I reported for work the following Saturday morning, I had to learn how to hold two cups in my left hand, while holding a plate or another cup in my right hand. Though I was clumsy and nervous for the first few days, I somehow managed to get through them; the only mishap I had was when I tried to hold three glasses in my left hand and another two in the right. A glass of water tipped over and spilled on a customer. I was frightened and apologized profusely. He was a shoe repairman, and luckily his leather apron deflected most of the water. When he saw my sad face, he comforted me, saying no harm was done, and he smiled. Fortunately, Boss Deng was away.

In the following two weeks, I learned to make milkshakes, sodas, and banana splits. Mostly, I served coffee, donuts, strawberry shortcakes, and pies. When Mr. Deng made fresh coffee, he cracked an egg and threw the shell into the urn with the grounds to enhance the aroma of the coffee. Dirty dishes were washed by hand in the kitchen by an elderly little man from Hoi San, while the other two waitresses or I washed the glasses in the two stainless-steel sinks behind the lunch counter. Juice and sundae glasses were all neatly arranged on the shelf by the wall.

My friend the cook was an excellent pie maker, and I particularly liked his fresh apple pies made from scratch. For helping him in the kitchen, peeling apples, and doing other little chores, he would often save me a piece whenever he baked. Apple pie and a scoop of vanilla ice cream was probably the highlight of my work week, other than receiving my wage of twelve dollars cash.

Knowing how thrilled my Mother would be, I sent her a money order for $12, my first week's salary. My diary of 1952 recorded that my first week's tips of pennies, nickels, and dimes added up to $5.25, and I spent $4.99 to buy myself a gold-plated watch. Luckily, there was no sales tax at the time. Long after that watch ceased to function, I kept it in my drawer as a cherished keepsake. To this day, I have very fond memories of the fruits of my first job: the remittance to my mother, the watch, total earnings of over four hundred dollars, and the mouth-watering apple pie à la mode.

17

THE ROOMING HOUSE

Housing in Canada was very tight for many years after the Second World War. Renting out rooms in one's home was popular, serving the demand and supplementing one's income. A year before my arrival, my father had retired and bought the three-storey, semi-detached house on Beaty Avenue in the west end of Toronto. Our family lived in the apartment on the main floor, renting out seven rooms on the second and third floors. This business involved a lot of work and headaches, because tenants did not always pay or follow the rules. From 1951 to 1957, after my father died, I learned to deal with most of these problems, since my English had improved enough to communicate with the tenants. A wooden sign saying ROOM TO RENT was hung on the front porch of our house, and I was responsible for showing the rooms to potential tenants. To my chagrin, some people rang our doorbell at dinnertime or late in the evening. A few times some characters thought we were running a motel and wanted to rent for one night only. Our requirements were for a minimum rental of one week, a deposit, and a known place of employment.

At the front of the house, a heavy, dark walnut door led into a vestibule. There, a door to the right opened into our apartment; on the left, a separate entrance led to the upper floors. We had four double rooms on the second floor and three single rooms on the third floor. Each room on the second floor was equipped with a double bed, a chest of drawers, a desk, an armchair, and two wooden side chairs. An electric hotplate with two burners for minor cooking was available upon request. We supplied towels and linen, and we changed the bedsheets once a week. The three small rooms on the third floor each had a single bed, a chest of drawers, and a card table with two folding chairs. We generally had seven to eleven tenants, and one bathroom plus a separate lavatory on the second floor served them all. The inadequate washroom facilities often created problems in the morning, when tenants were in a hurry to get to work – or to school when we had college students renting during the school year. A few arguments broke out, which I had to mediate, and a couple of times we had to allow tenants to use our private bathrooms.

Every Friday afternoon, and occasionally on Saturdays, I helped Dai Ma clean and vacuum the whole house, from top to bottom, including the washrooms and bathtubs. There were no showers, so the big enamelled porcelain tub, resting on its four clawed feet, dirtied easily and required scrubbing; I liked to use Comet cleanser generously on the rings around the tub. We had hardwood floors throughout the house, and every few months I had to strip the wax, clean the wood with turpentine, apply a coat of hard wax by hand on my knees, and finally shine the wood with an electric polisher until the floor gleamed.

As Dai Ma got older and suffered some minor strokes, I took over more chores. One particular task that I hated was washing the linen and towels, because this was done in our basement. It had a low ceiling and bare, grey cement walls and was rather dank and dark. I had not known any basements in China; to me it was like walking into a dungeon, and I had always been afraid of the dark and shadows. Like most Chinese children, I had heard too many stories about body- and soul-snatching ghosts. These evil spirits lurked in darkness, ready to pounce on me. My nerves were always on edge whenever I had to go by myself to the cellar at night, to change a fuse or do the laundry. First, I flipped a switch to turn on the forty-watt frosted bulb to light the front half of the basement; in the back half, I had to grope for the piece of string suspended from the low ceiling that snapped on another naked forty-watt bulb. The cellar was a scary place, and my heart always palpitated when I entered it at night. On some occasions when I had to wash and scrub my own underwear and socks on a washing board in a tub in the basement, I made sure there was daylight coming through the two small windows.

Rents, ranging from ten dollars to eighteen dollars per room, were collected each weekend, or else Dai Ma and I had to hunt for the tenants early the following week, before one or other of them spent their entire paycheque on booze or partying. I hated to chase after people for money. I hated even more opening the front door in the middle of the night for some drunken tenants and helping them up the stairs to their rooms. On one occasion, the police came.

One Saturday, a few minutes past midnight, an inebriated couple not only lost their keys and woke me to open their doors, but they also swore loudly and argued. I tried to cajole them to quiet down and go to bed, but they continued their fracas. The windows were open because of the heavy humidity, and our neighbour across the narrow alley, Miss Lyttle, became so agitated and angry that she called the police. The officer came and threatened to haul the couple off to jail if they didn't cease and desist. It was nearly two o'clock when, finally, all was quiet. Since I was all wound up and couldn't fall back to sleep, I decided to study. I had to write some very important Ontario Departmental Exams the following week. My university admission was at stake, and my fate depended on getting good grades.

Deep into the night I studied. For a breather, I laid my head on my folded arms, which were resting on the desk. I saw myself slumped in my armchair, the one my father used to sit in reading his *Sing Wah Daily*. I was crying, holding in my hands the report from the Ontario Department of Education. I had failed to pass English Composition and Literature. I could not stop the flow of tears, because my dream of going to university was dashed, but suddenly I felt something resting on my left shoulder. I turned my head and heard my father's voice behind me. He said "Ah Lun, don't cry. You'll be fine; I'll be with you. Go to bed now." I twisted my body toward the voice, but saw nothing. I got up and staggered to my bed.

Of the nearly one hundred tenants we had over the years that I lived in our rooming house, I remembered most vividly a tenant on the third floor. He was called Indian Jake, because of his Aboriginal heritage. He worked as a garbage collector, and I always opened the window wide whenever I entered his room for housekeeping. In the winter, when opening the window wide was not an option, I wore a cotton mask and smeared a dab of Tiger Balm ointment under my nose. He was friendly and often gave me a quarter as a tip for tidying his room or for calling him to answer the phone in our apartment. We had the only telephone in the building, and it was a party line, which meant we shared the line with another family somewhere in our district, a common practice at the time to save money.

Indian Jake had a pile of girlie magazines on his desk. As a curious teenager, I was most fascinated by the display of feminine charms, even though the most intriguing parts of the voluptuous ladies were blacked out or covered with pasties. Still, I appreciated looking at the photos; it beat looking at ladies wearing Maiden Form bras in the Eaton's catalogue. Those were the days before *Playboy* came on the scene and exhibited total nudity.

At age fifteen, I became something of a homemaker. I learned from Dai Ma and Dorothy how to clean and vacuum and to wash and iron clothes, mostly my own clothing. I sometimes cooked simple dinners, such as steamed rice, Chinese sausage, or steamed minced pork, boiled green beans, or stir-fried tofu and vegetables. As Dai Ma was not able to do very much in her later years, most days I hurried home after school and shopped for groceries. I did most of the cooking and washing, the renting of rooms, and the rent collection. I assumed ever more responsibilities, and there was less time for fun.

In the spring of 1956, Dai Ma was stricken with a massive and fatal stroke. I mourned her passing. Although we were not close, we did help each other. She had raised me for six years, and I was a companion for her. Living a short time with my father and my six years with Dai Ma was not particularly memorable at the time, but eventually I would develop more respect for them. They had earned the esteem of relatives and friends by their work ethic and helpfulness, and I realized that they had done their best to nurture me. I certainly owed them a debt, although at the time I was often resentful, too young to appreciate their efforts or express my love and respect for them.

Renting out rooms was definitely a chore I hated, but I tolerated it because it had helped pay our mortgage. The rooming house proved to be very useful; it taught me accounting, entrepreneurship, human nature, and housekeeping.

18

TORONTO'S CHINATOWN IN THE FIFTIES

Toronto's old Chinatown held a certain fascination for me from the very first time that my father took me there. To this young immigrant fresh off the boat, this town, centred on Elizabeth Street, which ran south to Queen from Dundas, between Bay and University, was a mysterious labyrinth of restaurants, herbal shops, homes, kung-fu clubs, grocery stores, gambling joints, and much more. This Chinese hub has largely disappeared now, because most of the people and businesses have moved westward to Spadina and Dundas. Huge influxes of Chinese immigrants in the past few decades have now created several Chinatowns scattered all over the Greater Toronto area and into surrounding municipalities.

In the late 1950s, the city of Toronto would expropriate the lower half of Chinatown to make way for the New City Hall, but a few of the established businesses on the north section of Elizabeth Street, such as Mon Kwok Trading Company, Lichee Garden, Lotus Garden, and Kwong Chow

Restaurant remained for many more years. Ho Sai Gai, the restaurant on Albert Street that employed me in 1953, has now been replaced by part of Toronto City Hall and Nathan Phillips Square. The Chinese United Church on Chestnut Street where I used to go is now occupied by a big hotel, The Metropolitan. My dental school on Edward Street was built on land once occupied by Chinese families and laundries.

Along Queen Street there were some dubious establishments, such as pawn shops, beer parlours, and fortune tellers. Often, I saw gypsies sitting in their windows beckoning to passersby to come in to have their palms read, to consult crystal balls, and for more exotic entertainments, especially for men. On the south side of Queen Street, opposite the site of the present-day City Hall, was the famous theatre called The Casino. I was told it used to feature legendary burlesque queens such as Sally Rand and Gypsy Rose Lee. In the fifties, when I got off the Queen streetcar to go to work, I could see people lining up to enjoy such entertainers as Johnny Ray, Liberace, and Eddie Fisher. Occasionally the Chinese community would rent this theatre for Cantonese opera or other special events.

On the west side of Elizabeth Street there were two poultry shops side by side, selling live chickens. This is where my father purchased the chicken that welcomed me to Toronto. The Wassermans, the two Jewish brothers who owned the shops, frequently stood by their doors, speaking a few words in fractured Chinese and openly competing for our business. According to my father, before the Chinese came to this neighbourhood, it was a Jewish settlement, part of the famous Ward. When Father was ill, and I went several times by myself to buy live chickens, the Wassermans would kill and clean them for an extra fifty cents. It was rather unpleasant going into those smelly shops, but I discovered that the meat did taste much better than that bought in local grocery stores.

A few stores away from the Wassermans were two of my favourite shops, the Kee Hong and Siu Yuen barbeques. I often stopped outside their windows to inhale the mouth-watering aroma and admire the golden-brown ducks and huge roasted pigs hung on big metal hooks. If I had money, I would often go into the Siu Yuen to buy half a duck or a slice of roasted pig, my favourite meat since childhood. Uncle Yue Sook was the owner and a good friend of my father's, so he frequently threw in for free a succulent pig's foot, so I could make rice congee with it.

The streets around Chinatown were full of life. When I walked by on a summer day, I often stopped to say hello and listen. Chinese elders, mostly men, sat in little groups on doorsteps, talking in sing-song voices. They recounted in the Sze Yup dialects the pathos of their home villages, exulted in the achievements of their children in Canada or China, and argued over whether Chiang Kai-shek would ever retake the mainland from the Communists. From open windows, I could hear Cantonese opera or the clicking of mah-jong tiles, or smell the fragrance of food sizzling in woks in a medley of exotic aromas. Children played happily in the streets and alleys, their laughter and chatter mingling with the jingle of wind chimes; I might have to kick a ball or throw a paper airplane back at them.

The houses and other buildings were mostly two or three stories, tightly packed together. Many were occupied by single men, sojourners who had immigrated to Canada in the early twentieth century. They were unable to get their families into Canada because of the discriminatory laws or economic constraints. Some, like my father, made modest fortunes from decades of hard work and could afford to bring their families to Canada, but many languished in lonely little houses and died, never returning to their homeland.

Chinatown had many of the clan associations, called Tongs, which were primarily based on family names or geographical areas of origin. A tong was typically located in a house or a small building, with a big room on the main floor for meetings and social activities. The rooms upstairs were used by members and as a hostel for folks coming from out of town to visit, or to see herbal doctors and medical specialists.

The Ho Sai Gai on Albert Street was the restaurant in Chinatown where I first worked. It had seats for a hundred and twenty people and served both Westernized and authentic Cantonese cuisine. This usually meant such dishes as egg rolls, chop suey, chow mein, and sweet-and-sour spareribs for most Western patrons. The connoisseurs and the Cantonese might order bird's-nest soup and braised abalone. At the time, these last two delicacies were relatively inexpensive compared to the astronomical prices of today. Patrons from theatres on Yonge Street, Bay Street, and The Casino on Queen Street were a major part of our clientele.

Many Japanese-Canadian couples had their wedding receptions at our restaurant. We had set menus of three, four, or five dollars per person. They sang, laughed, and really enjoyed themselves. I befriended several of them, and heard some of their stories about life during the war, when the Canadian government had forced them to move from the Pacific coast to camps in the interior of Canada. I could understand their suffering, and I empathized with them.

On Sundays for lunch we were only one of a few places that served dim sum, or "little hearts," made up of minced meat, shrimp, vegetables, and wrappings of rice. The variety and tastes of these delicacies were very limited then compared to the quality and huge selections of dim sum now served daily in hundreds of Toronto restaurants.

Above our restaurant was a small hotel called The New World. A long-time tenant, Mr. Chiang, frequently came down from his room to eat with his wife, but he also occasionally called for takeout, and I would deliver it to his room. Mrs. Chiang was very pretty and looked far younger than her husband. One late evening, I delivered to Mr. Chiang's room, but this time I was met by a young woman with flaming red hair. Later, when I asked Uncle Choi, an older waiter and accountant, where Mrs. Chiang had gone, I was told that she was not really his wife, just his companion for the past few months, and that she had now gone off with a richer man.

The foreign woman was called a Kuai Nui, whom Mr. Chiang had called for the night. Uncle Choi also explained that most of the men working in our restaurant had no families in Canada; therefore, they sometimes had to pay for female companionship. He refused to answer any more of my questions, and no one in my family or in my school had ever explained to me about the Yin and Yang. He teased me about wanting to know too much too soon.

One day our restaurant had a brush with the law when we were raided by the police at two o'clock in the morning. The cops told us that we were selling whisky illegally, because we did not have a liquor licence. At that time, it was extremely difficult to obtain or buy a licence, so the boss had us disguise the whisky in little teapots. The officers had posed as an ordinary couple coming in after a late-night movie to get chow mein and a "medicinal tea." We were caught serving them cups of Johnny Walker and Canadian Club. They told us no one was to leave, but as they were busy questioning the boss, I snuck out the kitchen door without taking time to put on my winter boots. I ran like a scared rabbit, because I didn't want to be charged as an accomplice to a crime. I huffed and puffed to reach Queen and Bay, and waited nervously while the Arctic wind and blizzard stung my face. My ears and toes were frozen and hurting, but I considered myself lucky to have escaped and avoided having a criminal record. I learned the next day that the boss and the waiter who had served the couple had been taken to the police station and formally charged. They appeared in court and paid a hefty fine.

On another occasion, I delivered food to a gambling den on the second floor of a building on Chestnut Street. As I entered the guarded entrance, my ears were assailed by a cacophony of talking and swearing and the clicking of mah-jong tiles. The parlour had a big fan-tan table, with a crowd standing around it. I watched briefly as the boss lifted a metal shaker off the pile of buttons and, with a curved stick, began parting them four by four. The men who guessed how many buttons would be left – one, two, three, or four – would be the winners, depending on how they had bet. In a side room, four men were shuffling mah-jong tiles and then piling them in neat rows. The windows were shut and the drapes were drawn, because gambling was subjected to raids by the police. My eyes itched because the air was choked with smoke. I ran out as quickly as I could, and the foul air chased me like a spirit. A consolation for me was that I got a big tip – a two-dollar bill and some change.

After working four years at the Ho Sai Gai, I applied and got a summer job in 1957 at Lotus Garden, an upscale restaurant with a liquor licence, which meant patrons spent more in food, alcohol, and gratuities. I made about one-third more than I had previously. The owners there belonged to the clan with the family names of Lew, Quan, Cheng, and Chu. This association was called Lung Kong. These folks usually did not employ anyone who did not belong to the four families. Fortunately, I was acquainted with part owners Jimmy Lew and Jeffery Chu, who were kind enough to make an exception.

The summer after my first year of university in 1958, I was lucky to be hired to work at the very famous Lichee Garden, thanks mainly to Mr. Harry Lim, majority owner and a friend of my Uncle Joe Lowe. He was a prominent Chinese leader who was sympathetic to poor students like me. This restaurant was the largest and grandest in Chinatown, established in 1948. It boasted a huge dining room and a smaller banquet room. Total seating capacity was more than three hundred, and the restaurant was nearly always full on weekends. A three-man band played popular and dancing music. Two uniformed Caucasian commissionaires were stationed at the grand entrance. The whole place looked chic and expensive. A large segment of the patrons were Jewish, as ads were placed in Jewish as well as mainstream Toronto newspapers. Jewish people are generally very knowledgeable about Chinese food. They always expected good food and service; they also tipped more generously than most other people, especially when they knew that I was a poor college student. I made many good friends with them; a few also became my colleagues after I graduated from dentistry.

I enjoyed working at Lichee Garden, because the patrons were mostly sophisticated, well-to-do, and generous, but I had to work very hard. As the youngest waiter working only for the summer, I was assigned to the tables farthest from the kitchen. Sometimes, I had to run to make sure the soups were still hot when I got to the diners. My hours of work changed a lot, some days starting in the morning and finishing in the late afternoon, other days starting at five o'clock in the afternoon and ending well past two in the morning. Some Fridays and Saturdays I had to work until closing around three in the morning. Sleeping was not easy with the many changes in schedule every week. However, the money was very good, and I counted myself lucky that I made enough to pay for my second year's tuition at dental school.

Some very interesting people dined at Lichee Garden, such as Speaker of the House of Commons from the district of St. Paul, The Honourable Roland Michener, who later became the Governor General of Canada. He was a scholar and a gentleman, who talked to me a bit about Canadian history, sports, and politics. Entertainers and Hollywood movie stars came, but the most exotic personality I met was a burlesque queen. On one late Saturday night, a glamorous lady with striking red hair swept into our dining room with her entourage. I do not remember the lady's name; possibly it was Blaze Starr, who was very famous for her exotic burlesque show. She drew everyone's attention as our band played a raunchy number. She wriggled her hips, waved, and blew kisses in every direction.

A few days later a group of waiters gave a stag party for a fellow worker soon to be married to a C.O.D., a mail-order bride from Hong Kong, and they dragged me along to the Victory Theatre at the corner of Dundas and Spadina. We sat near the front of the stage, in eager anticipation. First the

Master of Ceremonies came on stage, and for about half an hour he told jokes and tap-danced. He was actually not bad at all. Then with much fanfare and cheers, the burlesque queen was introduced. She pranced onto the stage with the spotlight following her every move. Her voluptuous body was concealed by two large fans of feathers, which she waved demurely across her body, flashing glimpses of feminine pulchritude.

The sexy lady recognized our group from the restaurant and called out greetings enthusiastically! She danced superbly, exotic and alluring without being crude, compared to the nude dancers these days. The boys said that she performed with more abandon that day than the laws of morality permitted at the time. I was mesmerized; I could not see whether she was wearing any panties or a G-string, as required by law. Toronto was known then to be prudish. For me, the show was eye-popping and more exhilarating than anything I had ever seen in my young life. In subsequent months, I did go very willingly with the boys to see several more shows at the Victory.

In the late fifties, a large new restaurant called Kwong Chow opened on Elizabeth Street near Dundas. Almost immediately, it became a very popular eatery, mainly because its owners, Jean Lumb and her husband, Doyle Lumb, were charming hosts. Jean, in particular, had a dynamic personality and was a prominent leader and activist for the Chinese-Canadian communities throughout the country. I talked with her a number of times and found her to be very caring and helpful. Her son Douglas Lumb and I were friends, as we often met at Chinese student functions at the University of Toronto.

Toronto's Chinatown in the mid-twentieth century, while small and cozy compared to today's many larger Chinatowns scattered around the Greater Toronto area, offered colourful history, culture, exotic food, and some fantastic stories from a wide variety of people. Restaurants were the most important business in Chinatown, its economic engine. In the years that I worked there, I matured, learned many lessons, came of age, and appreciated its uniqueness.

19

CHINESE CUISINE

Food has always played an extraordinary role in Chinese history and culture – and for me personally. My experience with hunger in my youth taught me a deep appreciation for food, especially good food, and a disdain for any abuse or wastefulness. My mother had taught me to imagine how much labour went into a bowl of rice: a farmer bending over planting young seedlings while barefooted, walking behind a water buffalo pulling a heavy iron plough, praying to the Thunder God for rain if there were drought, spreading smelly and worm-infested "night soil" as fertilizer, cutting, harvesting, and so much more. I had watched my mother painstakingly but lovingly wrap rice in broad bamboo leaves before boiling them for hours to make jungg. I had watched chefs spend hours preparing hor yip fon: steamed rice with minced meat wrapped in lotus leaves. I have learned that each food ingredient has its own innate flavour and can be synergistically enhanced with some imagination and skill. When foodstuffs are available, the Chinese can really use their ingenuity to create marvellous dishes fit for an emperor. I appreciate fine food when prepared with loving care.

My initiation into Chinese cuisine began in my teens, when I was working in Chinatown. Frequently, I took time to explain to Western patrons the Chinese name, the ingredients, and even the history of the dishes that I was serving them, such as the origin of bird's-nest soup and chop suey. The extra service usually earned me an additional quarter in tips, enough to go occasionally to a matinee movie on a Saturday before I reported for work. I learned about these things by going into the kitchen in my spare time to watch the chefs and to ask questions. They were at first rather reluctant to talk to a pipsqueak like me, but I earned their friendship by smiling a lot and getting them cups of tea or coffee.

They taught me the basic techniques, the art and the philosophy of Chinese cooking. On some occasions when the restaurant was not too busy, they allowed me to cook some simple dishes for customers. I even tried cooking with two woks at the same time. At the beginning my hands were too slow, and some delicate vegetables, such as snow peas, got a little burnt. Vegetables should be quickly cooked to retain their natural texture and lush colours. I was told that overcooking is a sin. Fortunately for me, none of the customers complained about the few dishes that I cooked. Some of them even returned the following weeks for more!

Because of the vast geographical and ethnic diversity of China, huge varieties of cuisine exist; the most famous throughout the country and the world is the cuisine of the Cantonese, with which I am most familiar. Canton, the large city near Hong Kong where I was born, now known as Guangzhou, is the capital of the province of Guangdong, which includes Hong Kong. This vast area can draw on the coastal waters of the South China Sea and the large estuary of the Pearl River delta. These waterways are teeming with fish, fowl, and other aquatic creatures. All are tasty by themselves, but they can easily be enhanced by a dash of soy sauce, a sprinkle of ginger, green onion, or any other ingredients a cook can dream of. Freshness is paramount. At a farewell dinner in Hong Kong, I saw a sea bass swimming in a tank; within half an hour it was served on our platter with sweet-and-sour sauce, and I also enjoyed the molluscs stir-fried with black-bean paste, ginger, and garlic.

We Chinese will eat anything that nature has to offer. Frequent famines taught us to be resourceful and creative, certainly not picky in our choices. From the mountains come delicacies such as bird's-nest soup and pheasants, from the oceans come crabs and abalone, and from local ponds and rivers come the vast varieties of fish, molluscs, and shrimps. Fresh vegetables and fruits from the land are essential parts of the meal, while desserts are optional and often not served at the table.

In selecting the menu and preparing the dishes, many Chinese pay attention to the ancient philosophy of the balance of nature based on the Taoist concept of Yin and Yang. Yin is soft, cool, and feminine, while Yang is hard, hot, and masculine. They complement each other in nature as well as in the kitchen. For my mother, too much fire and vigour, like fried food, would cause *yeet hay* – yang fire that can give you heartburn, bad breath, and canker sores. Yin and Yang should blend in balance, according to many Cantonese chefs.

I was fortunate to have some instructions in cooking from two good teachers. I learned some Canadian cooking, such as roasted turkey and spaghetti and meat sauce when I was working at the High Park Grill. I learned Chinese cooking from the head chef of the Ho Sai Gai Restaurant, master chef Chow Yet-tien. I still remember a few of the dishes that Mr. Chow taught me.

Gung bo guy ding, is made up of chicken, vegetables, and roasted almonds or cashews. The meat of the chicken is diced, marinated, and then stir-fried in a wok with such vegetables as green peppers, celery, onions, water chestnuts, bamboo shoots, and mushrooms. Cashews or almonds, previously lightly boiled and then deep-fried, are sprinkled on top of the dish. For myself, I like to add a few red chili peppers to the mix, to spice it like a Szechwan dish.

I love steamed minced pork; pork is perhaps the most popular meat dish in China, because pigs are easy to care for, cheap to feed, and they can live anywhere. As a child, I raised my piglet on boiled pumpkin, any spare vegetables, and the peelings of fruits and yams. In Mr. Chow's kitchen, I used a heavy cleaver to chop and mince the pork into a fine paste, to which I added chopped water chestnuts, black mushrooms, and salted fish. For dinner, I could eat two large bowls of rice with this dish and nothing else!

Dim sum is my favourite for lunch, and this consists of dozens of varieties of small delicacies, from braised chicken feet and curried squid to fried won tons. My favourite is har gow, which I sometimes helped Mr. Chow make for special dim sum lunches, which were available only on Sundays in the 1950s. A har gow is made with a thin wrapping of rice flour, stuffed with minced pork, water chestnuts, and bits of shrimp, and then steamed in a big wok. In those days dim sum were neither as sophisticated as they are now in Toronto, nor available every day. The har gows we made were big, lumpy, and had very little shrimp in them, but they still tasted great to me. In the summers, when I didn't need to worry about homework, I sometimes went to my restaurant extra early on Sundays to watch the chefs and help a bit around the kitchen. Mr. Chow was very good to me, often sharing with me the first batch of dim sum that he steamed.

Spring rolls were another of my favourite dim sum dishes. Mr. Chow showed me how to place his previously cooked filling onto the centre of a flour wrapper, fold it, and roll it into a sausage shape approximately one inch by four inches. The filling was made of strips of barbecued pork, bean sprouts, mushrooms, green onions, celery, and bits of shrimp. The very first time that I tried to deep fry them in a bath of very hot oil, I had a little accident. Instead of sliding a roll gently into the oil, I dropped the first one from a little too high, and several drops of scalding oil splattered onto my hand. My skin bubbled. Luckily, Mr. Chow had some Chinese herbal wine to smear on my hand to soothe it and help the healing. Nowadays, vegetable oil is mostly used for deep frying, but back then we used lard, which held a much higher temperature and was supposed to enhance the flavour.

Another chef explained to me that a well-prepared dish should appeal to all the five senses. I think the humble spring roll that I mentioned above is a good example. A spring roll should smell fragrant when it comes out of its hot, oily bath, should look golden brown like a sunbathed beauty, reveal a light, delicate texture when touched by the tongue, sound crunchy when your teeth sink into it, and taste fantastic!

In the twentieth century, chop suey was the Chinese dish that North Americans knew best. From 1953 to 1958, when I worked as a waiter after school or during the summer, I served a lot of chop suey. It was a best-selling item, and helped greatly to fund my college education. Now, chop suey is most often listed in menus as stir-fried mixed vegetables. I think the name was changed because Chinese food has improved tremendously in both variety and quality, and due to the large influx of Chinese immigrants to Canada and the United States, the choice of Chinese dishes is unlimited. Consequently, the humble chop suey has yielded its popularity to more sophisticated dishes. However, I like it and I cook it.

The origin of chop suey is a culinary mystery. One account says that it was invented by Chinese pioneers working on the transcontinental railroads in America, and favoured American tastes by using less spice and local produce. Another story is that a prime minister named Li Hong Zhang of the Manchu Qing Dynasty visited the United States in 1896, and while in San Francisco, he ate in a local restaurant. He was served chop suey and found it a delightful dish, declaring it refreshingly different from the exotic everyday fare of a high Mandarin such as himself! From then on, this no-name dish became famous throughout the Western World.

Chop suey means "bits and pieces." In the restaurants that I worked in, I observed that the ingredients included chopped celery, carrots, mushrooms, onions, and lots of bean sprouts. Meats, such as chicken, beef, or shrimp could be added. My mother's version of it was to stir-fry whatever vegetables were available in a wok; she called it, in the Xin Hui dialect, chop choi, meaning "mixed greens." In wartime, that was often all we had to eat, with maybe a little rice, but seldom any meat. She cooked it with scraps of vegetables that farmers had thrown out or those that could be bought cheaply, such as Chinese cabbage, mustard greens, and onions. However, in peacetime, she usually added chicken to a mixture of snow peas, water chestnuts, bean sprouts, and mushrooms. For my twelfth-birthday celebration in the summer of 1949, the year that I left my beloved home in Guangzhou for Canada, my mother prepared her special chop choi. She also added a steamed fish, a leg of barbecued goose, and bird's-nest soup. I will never forget that supper. It would take eight years before my mother cooked it again, on my request, for my twentieth birthday dinner, this time in Toronto. One minor change in the menu was duck instead of goose.

I used to cook a lot of chop suey or a variation of it for dinner, because it was easy to prepare and inexpensive, and I needed to add only a little meat for the protein and extra flavour. I could easily change this versatile dish to one called guy ding by mixing in a handful of roasted almonds, or to chow mein by adding chop suey to a plate of pan-fried noodles. I loved them all.

Food is a dominant part of Chinese culture. Its meticulous cultivation, preparation, experimentation, and cooking styles have elevated Chinese cuisine to the highest level of sophisticated international cuisine, and more than thirty million Chinese scattered around the globe have introduced it to the world. In almost every Chinese restaurant that I go to in the West, I can see many Western families, young and old, using chopsticks. I am pleased that I have learned some Chinese cooking, and introduced it to many of my Western friends. Once upon a time, I even thought about going into the Chinese restaurant business. These days, with hundreds of Chinese restaurants serving excellent food in Toronto, I look forward to dining out and sampling the distinctive cuisines of many regions, such as Sichuan, Shanghai, Beijing, and, of course, Guangzhou. We Cantonese rightfully claim that our cuisine is the best in China and in America, for its huge variety and new recipes.

20

MAN'S WORST FEAR

My mother once quoted the following old Chinese saying to me: "A man's worst fear is entering the wrong line of work; a woman's is marrying the wrong man." I don't believe this quote is true today, because men and women are working equally. However, I remembered that warning when I was a senior in high school and was planning for the future: would I go to university, learn a trade, be a technician, or go into the restaurant business?

Mr. Choy, a partner of the Ho Sai Gai where I worked, had taught me much about the restaurant business. I listened to him carefully, because I thought that I would never go hungry if I were to run an eatery. He was the assistant manager and accountant. Thinking of retirement, he offered to train me to take over his position and his shares in the company. The cost was about five to six thousand dollars. While I had a little over one thousand dollars saved, the rest I could have borrowed from a Chinese Credit Union, managed by the Gee Dug Tong; its treasurer was my cousin Joe Jen, who had always been helpful to me.

Although the Chinese population in Toronto was fewer than five thousand in 1957, most Chinese, Japanese, or other Canadians who wanted authentic Chinese food would go to Chinatown. "Let's have Chinese," was becoming a popular suggestion with the ever-expanding population in the city and the suburbs. Mr. Choy's other partners were also getting old; the chances were good that, within a few years, I could become the sole owner if I worked hard. It was a tempting offer.

When I wrote to ask my mother if I should go into the restaurant business, she immediately replied in part, "Have you forgotten, before you went to Canada, why I bought you two big dictionaries, one in Chinese and the other in English and Chinese, and paid someone to teach you the alphabet and a little English? It was so you could get ahead quickly in the New World. Formal schooling was not possible for me, but university is the future for you, to be somebody. The way I speak, my accent, and my poor family background are burdens that I have suffered all my life. You go study; don't worry about bringing me to Canada. I can endure the wait!"

Her words immediately made me think seriously about what profession I should pursue at university. I started to study even harder so that I could pass my Grade 13 exams with good enough grades to get into the University of Toronto. In the 1950s, it was the only university in the city and I could not afford to go to an out-of-town school.

At that time, a passing grade of B in the Ontario Grade 13 departmental examinations was the bare minimum required for acceptance to the university. I wrote nine exams: Physics, Chemistry, Algebra, Geometry, Trigonometry, French Composition and Literature, and English Composition and Literature. They were very difficult, each taking two and a half hours. Furthermore, the exam questions were made up and marked by teachers outside our school, and we could not guess what topics would be covered or what questions were most likely to be asked. We all dreaded those exams, because so much was riding on the results. I was apprehensive.

June 1957 was abnormally hot. Temperatures were well above 90°
Fahrenheit for many days; high humidity added to our discomfort. Sleep
was difficult, and I had to take some sleeping pills. Air conditioning was
very rare in most places, and we didn't have it at home or at school. Con-
centrating on my studies was also extremely difficult, because my sister had
given birth to her son, Rodney, that spring. He would cry when hungry or
wet, and his crib was right next to my room!

I had some ideas about what I wanted to study. I thought about
becoming an engineer like my older brother, Howard, but my inclination
was toward the health sciences, and I had not forgotten what I told my
Grade 7 class: I wanted to be a dentist. When I talked to my favourite
high-school teachers, Miss Campbell, who was my Grade 13 home-room
teacher, and Mr. Wanless, they told me that I had the empathy, aptitude,
and social skills needed to be a good health professional. They suggested
that I look into both medicine and dentistry.

I went to see Professor Campbell at the Banting Institute on College
Street, who was recommended to me by his sister Miss Campbell. Dr.
Campbell was a soft-spoken man in his fifties, who was teaching physiology
at the University of Toronto's Faculty of Medicine. He talked to me about
practising medicine, medical research, and teaching.

I was acquainted with two dentists. One was Dr. James Toi Hing, a
friend of my brother-in-law with whom I had gone fishing a couple of times.
He was very enthusiastic about dentistry and urged me to apply to McGill
University in Montreal, his alma mater. The other dentist was Dr. Mullet,
director of clinical admissions at the Faculty of Dentistry. I had met him
a few times at the restaurant where I worked. He had been a missionary
to China and had taught dentistry at the Wah Sai University in Chendu,
before returning to Canada after the Communists came to power and
made foreigners unwelcome. When I met him at the dental school at 230
College Street, he spoke Mandarin to me, but quickly switched to English

when he remembered my dialect was mainly Cantonese. He took me on a tour of the clinics and allowed me to watch students doing extractions and fillings. The sight of blood did not bother me at all, although the shrill sound of the drill was a bit disconcerting.

Both medicine and dentistry appealed to me, because I liked the idea of being a doctor, able to help people. Also, I thought it was an excellent way to earn a living, which was a very important consideration, because I needed to support myself and my mother as soon as possible. Getting my mother out of China was an urgent matter. I was anxious because the mainland was undergoing tremendous political upheavals and life was getting more hazardous every day, with rumours of widespread famine. Therefore, time and economics became the critical factors in my decision of which health profession to choose.

Back then medicine took a minimum of seven years and dentistry a year less, beyond Grade 12, not counting the extra years for possible specialization. Government loans and bursaries were extremely limited and difficult to obtain; I had to rely on myself entirely.

To get my mother to Canada I needed $700 to buy her a false identity paper and passport. I was not qualified to sponsor her, because of the very restrictive immigration laws for the Chinese at that time. Also, due to the circumstances of my birth and the false name listed in my passport, I had not dared to apply for Canadian citizenship. Airfare to Toronto was nearly a thousand dollars, which was very expensive. Travel by boat would have been cheaper, but, because my mother was very prone to motion sickness, I did not want her to suffer. I was also worried about her living expenses after arrival. Employment was an important issue for me. Dentists were in great demand at the time, because of a shortage. Besides, my friend Dr. Hing said he had more patients than he could handle, and gave me an open invitation to join him as an associate dentist upon graduation.

After much thought, I finally chose dentistry, partly because I knew I was a worrier by nature, and I was concerned that the life-and-death issues inherent in the practice of medicine might be too stressful for me. I made only one application, to the University of Toronto, and, after an interview with the faculty secretary and several anxious weeks of waiting, I finally received my letter of admission from the university. That day, I celebrated my good news by going to a matinee movie, *The Bridge on the River Kwai*, starring William Holden and Alec Guinness.

21

GINGER TEA FOR MOTHER

After nearly eight years of separation, at last my mother and I were to be reunited in Canada. Had it really been that long since our parting at the ocean terminal in Kowloon, Hong Kong? In December 1949, I had been a boy of twelve, about to be separated from my mother for the first time in my life. That afternoon she had insisted that I wear a woollen cap and a wool sweater for the voyage, even though it was a mild day with an overcast sky. Blinking back her tears, her voice cracking, she again reminded me to write often, study hard, and make sure to keep warm in the land of freezing winters that she called, *kar na dai*.

At that turbulent time, many people feared that another world war might soon erupt between communist and capitalist countries, because rumours were spreading that North Korea was preparing to attack South Korea. We both wondered, when – or if – we would ever see each other again.

The Lord worked His wonders for us, because now, in October 1957, my mother was scheduled to arrive. I paced anxiously outside the Royal York Hotel in downtown Toronto, waiting for the airport bus. After half an hour waiting impatiently, and constantly peering through the fog for any large headlights approaching, I walked back into the hotel to ask the Air Canada agent why it was taking so long for the bus from Buffalo to reach Toronto. He answered that it had been fortunate that the pilot was able to land in Buffalo at all, because for the entire evening heavy fog had shrouded not only the airport but also the Queen Elizabeth Highway to Toronto. "Don't worry, young fella. It'll be here soon; Buffalo is only one hundred miles away," he added.

"Easy for him to say," I muttered as I went outside again. He did not know that my mother was travelling alone in an airplane for the first time and did not know any English or how to fill out immigration papers. And there was also that problem with acute motion sickness.

Finally, nearly half an hour past midnight, the bus arrived. As the passengers started to disembark, pandemonium broke out as loud greetings, laughing, and crying filled the quiet night. When I saw Mother walking down the steps hesitantly, looking here and there, I pushed past a noisy Cantonese family, to extend my hands to her.

She looked at me and asked, "*Ney hy ah suey*? Who are you?"

"I am Ah Lun. Don't you recognize me?"

"You are not Ah Lun. Are you?"

"I am Ah Lun, your son, born on the lunar month of June the 14th. Do you remember?"

"Ah, Ah Lun! You have grown so much!"

We fell into each other's arms and were silent for several seconds. Mother took out a handkerchief to wipe her eyes and her lips. She asked to go to the washroom, as she had thrown up twice, once on the plane and once on the bus.

Eventually, we arrived at home by taxi. I warmed up some food for her, but Mother ate only half of a small bowl of rice, with a bit of salted fish and slivers of ginger. She declined my offer of Campbell's chicken noodle soup, but requested some ginger tea. I made it by slicing nine thin pieces of fresh ginger root, then adding them to a pot of boiling water, along with a porcelain spoonful of honey. She eagerly drank her hot tea, eating the ginger as well. Minutes later, she said, "I am feeling better. The fire in this tea has warmed my liver and belly. Ginger is a good-luck food for me. Do you know that ginger was served at your one-month-old birthday party?"

"Oh yeah? You mean you fed me spicy ginger when I was only one month old?" I teased her.

"No. *Sor Jai*, silly boy. It was for the guests. I fed you my own milk!" Then she flashed me her biggest smile of the night. Gradually, a bit of colour came back to her face, and her voice sounded stronger. Not wanting to tire her too much with more questions about her trip, I showed her how the faucets worked for a warm bath. She soon changed into her blue flannel pyjamas and went to bed. I leaned over her and, for several seconds, my fingers stroked her soft, pale cheeks. I carefully tucked her in under the red wool blanket.

It was two-thirty in the morning when I finally went to my room. I kneeled by my bed and thanked the Lord for bringing my mother safely out of China and reuniting us. At last my dream had come true. With a smile on my face, I promptly fell asleep.

I was awakened suddenly to a baby's shrill cries, but within minutes it was quiet again as I heard my sister getting up to tend to six-month-old Rodney. I fell back to sleep until late morning. I walked into the kitchen and found my mother was already drinking tea and eating toast in the kitchen with my brother-in-law. Ed had made toast for my mother, and she said this was the first time she had eaten toast with butter and jam for breakfast; in China, she usually ate steamed buns and congee or Quaker's oatmeal.

I spent the rest of that Sunday showing Mother our house, particularly the kitchen and the pantry, where rice and Chinese foodstuffs were stored. Since Dorothy was preoccupied with the baby, and Ed worked in his restaurant most evenings, I was doing a fair amount of the cooking, and was anxious for Mother to take over my chores. It took her a while to learn how everything worked, because the equipment, methods, and ingredients in America were much different from those she had in China.

She had to learn how to use an electric stove and oven instead of burning wood, and a flat-bottomed frying pan instead of a wok for stir-frying. Our refrigerator was strange for her. It had frozen meats that needed defrosting, whereas the vast majority of homes in China did not have refrigeration. Cheese and sour cream smelled funny to her. Dorothy taught my mother how to make spaghetti, roasted turkey with stuffing, casseroles, and desserts, like puddings and cakes. After a few weeks, Mother said that she had never eaten so much meat and sweet food before, and that she was getting plump. I had noticed that her face looked smoother and rosier; even her hair appeared glossier and darker.

A few months after her arrival, I took her to my school for a dental checkup and radiographs. To my delight, she had a complete set of very good teeth, with no cavities, caps, or old fillings; all she needed was a thorough cleaning and removal of stains, although her teeth were somewhat worn due to the vigorous chewing of coarse food all her life, like brown rice and fresh meat that had not been tenderized or aged. (After about a year of living in North America and eating a softer diet, her next checkup would shock me; she had two cavities which needed fillings.)

Mother seemed to adjust well to the Canadian way of life, coping with the Arctic chill in her first winter and helping me to shovel snow. Frequently she was outdoors pushing Rodney's baby pram down Beaty Avenue to King Street for long walks, wearing earmuffs plus a wool hat. When she came in from the cold, Mother would say in her pidgin English, "Oh Bouy, verly, verly cold." Her taste in food became Canadian in a short time: she loved cheese, apple pie, turkey, hot dogs, and all manner of beef, whether minced, roasted, or barbecued. She regularly cooked potatoes instead of rice and western dishes like spaghetti and corned beef. I voluntarily paid Dorothy twenty dollars each month for the cost of my mother's food, because I wanted to support her.

She helped me greatly in the housekeeping chores like laundry and cleaning tenants' rooms. In her spare time, she liked watching variety programs like *The Ed Sullivan Show*, and laughed heartily with Red Skelton. She adapted well to living with a stepdaughter and family. Dorothy and Ed never uttered any complaints about Mother; I was greatly relieved, because I was worried about possible tensions with all of us living in close quarters.

Ed's restaurant was across the city in Scarborough, which took about three-quarters of an hour of driving each way, and, with another baby expected, they needed more room. When Ed and Dorothy decided in the spring of 1959 to sell the house and buy a bungalow on Manorwood Road in Scarborough, it was a relief for me. My share of the net proceeds amounted to a little less than three thousand dollars, most of which I would use to pay off the debt I had by then accrued to bring my mother from China to Canada.

When our old house on Beaty Avenue was put on the market, I started looking for a place to rent for Mother and me. With a very tight budget, I had limited options. Besides looking in the newspapers, I actually put an ad in the *Toronto Daily Star*: "University of Toronto student and mother, Orientals, seeking to rent an apartment at a discount, in exchange for doing household chores like gardening, snow removal, running errands, and other light duties. Please call." I had in mind that an elderly person or couple might be interested in such arrangement. Several persons responded; one was looking for a superintendent for an apartment building, another couple wanted home care for aged parents, and one woman was looking for a maid and part-time houseboy. None of these offers appealed to me, so I checked the papers every day and walked the streets downtown, anxiously in search of something acceptable, since we had to vacate our house by June 30 when the sale was due to close.

Finally, I found a small one-bedroom flat on Spadina Road near Dupont; it was the front half of the second floor of an older house. It had a small kitchen, but we had to share the bathroom in the middle with the couple in the rear flat. Mother and I moved into this place on June 28, just in time. Mother insisted on giving me the bedroom, while she used a folding sofa in the living room. Before the sofa bed was built by a carpenter recommended to me by my cousin Joe Jen, my mother slept on the floor for a week. Our windows faced the street and, because of the summer heat, humidity, and lack of air conditioning or an electric fan, we kept the windows open. The sidewalk was only a few feet away, and a Spadina bus stop was close by; I could hear the squeaking sounds of the brakes and smell the exhaust fumes as the vehicle pulled away. Sometimes passengers talked as if they were half-deaf, even late at night. After several weeks of trying to adapt, I found sleep was hopeless, so I decided we had to move again. Luckily there was not any written lease; I only needed to give a month's notice.

About that time, I heard that a friend, Bob Chung, and his family were moving into a new apartment building in St. James Town, not too far from the university. When I talked to him, I found out that the rent was very reasonable, because the federal government had guaranteed a bank loan to the builder in exchange for some degree of rent control. I immediately went to investigate and discovered that there were still a few units left and that the rent was $96 a month, only $11 more than the flat on Spadina Road. That summer, Mother found a job working in a vegetable farm out in Mississauga, owned by Wu Bing, an acquaintance from our county of Sze Yup, so we could afford the extra cost.

On the Labour Day weekend of 1959, Mother and I moved into a one-bedroom apartment at 730 Ontario Street. From our windows on the twelfth floor, I could look across Bloor Street into Rosedale Valley and beyond. Among numerous tall trees I could see large, elegant homes, where affluent and well-known Torontonians lived, such as the president of the

University of Toronto, Dr. Claude Bissell. On many Sundays, I walked across the bridge at Bloor and Sherbourne and into Rosedale and admired the stately homes, their manicured lawns shaded by mature oaks and elms. How I wished that someday I could afford to live there.

Christmas Eve 1959 found us cosy in our new apartment on the twelfth floor. With an amused smile, Mother was helping me decorate a small Scotch pine that I had bought – at half-price, because it was near closing time. After I reached up to put a chain of little clear lights and a star on the treetop, Mother plugged it in. Instantly the room lit up, with all the lights shining brilliantly. Her eyes also sparkled in awe.

We had hardly any gifts to put under the tree. I gave Mother a box of Yardley's English lavender soap. She handed me a soft, warm bundle, tied with a red ribbon. It was six pairs of her hand-knitted socks.

With the Leslie Bell Singers carolling on the radio, and the aromatic fragrance of the pine tree permeating the whole living room, I felt very relaxed. For the first time in our lives, Mother and I were celebrating our Christmas together, just the two of us.

She prepared a sumptuous dinner of steamed chicken with black Chinese mushrooms and goose-liver sausage, winter melon with dried scallops, and bird's-nest soup. The expensive ingredients of the soup were parting gifts given to her by relatives in Hong Kong; she had saved them for very special occasions. To complement the dinner, we each had a small glass of Hennessey cognac; again, it was an item she had saved for the festive season.

After we had eaten, Mother made tea with chrysanthemum flowers and a spoonful of honey. We drank it while standing by the window, looking down on the houses and trees across the street, decorated in colourful lights and Christmas scenes. We saw tiny snowflakes dancing across the sky. It was a magical tableau.

I rested a hand gently on her shoulder and asked, "Mama, are you happy?"

She answered in Chinese, "*Ho hoi sum.* Very happy. We have our own home. We are together. We have a future."

Raising our porcelain cups, we wished each other a very Merry Christmas.

22

ST. JAMES TOWN

St. James Town was my "stomping ground," where my mother and I lived for six years. This "town" was bounded on the north by Bloor Street, on the south by Wellesley Street, and was sandwiched between Sherbourne and Parliament streets. The area had started out in the 1870s as a desirable middle-class neighbourhood with quaint Victorian houses. However, after the Second World War, it slowly deteriorated, strongly affected by the Great Depression of the 1930s. Sadly, by the 1950s, it had become a little slummy. However, living there was a positive experience for me.

Coming home from school, if the weather was fine and I had the time and wanted to save a fare, I would walk north on University Avenue from my dental school on Edward Street, east on Wellesley to Sherbourne, and then north to my home, which might take thirty-five minutes. Along the way I had many opportunities to see and hear interesting sights and sounds. On Sherbourne Street was the run-down-looking Selby Tavern, where on several occasions I saw an old unshaven man wearing a battered soldier's cap loitering by the doors, mumbling and saluting me as I passed by. In the evenings on the same corner, two or three ladies of the night might be standing and smiling at men. I skirted around them. Around Wellesley and Jarvis, I sometimes walked by gay couples and transvestites in colourful outfits.

Our building was also full of interesting people. One of them was a medical resident who loved to write and was well-versed in literature, philosophy, and music. I admired him and we sometimes had conversations covering many topics, as we drank green tea. We also talked about his heritage and the persecutions of the Jewish people by the Nazis, and how some twenty thousand of them escaped the Holocaust by fleeing to China, especially to Shanghai. When he became animated in a discussion, he sometimes forgot about time, and I had to remind him to hurry to his patients. His favourite reply was, "If a patient is destined to live, he'll live. If he is destined to die, he'll die. Not too much I can do except a few little things, like providing painkillers."

Tienny and Janet Wong were a young couple who lived three stories above us. Whenever I had some leisure time, I visited them to talk and to play mah-jong. There were often four people around who liked to play for small wagers, which was about the cost of going to a movie. At the time, I was dating a girl named Polly, who was a smart mah-jong player. Her lovely fingers would reach out sensually on the board to pick up a tile; she would caress it for a second or two. Then she'd take a quick glance at it before keeping or discarding it. She beat me and the other players most of the time. We would eventually break up, because I was still in school and not ready to commit to a serious relationship.

In the autumn of 1962, it would be my St. James Town friend Janet Wong and her sister Louise Mark who somehow got me interested in meeting a certain Chinese nurse working in my hospital. So St. James Town also played a romantic role in my life; it was an unforgettable part of my past.

23

A CRUSTY PROFESSOR

Professor Stewart "Sandy" MacGregor was a crusty and opinionated man, hated by some and loved by many others. He became a mentor. He would help me launch my career.

Entering my final year of dental school, I needed to decide what to do upon graduation. I had four choices: open a practice, which meant borrowing a large sum of money to set up, and running the risk of not having any patients; work for a busy, experienced dentist; go to Hong Kong and work in dental public health or a public dental clinic; or do an internship in a hospital. I preferred to stay in Toronto, because I did not want to leave my mother alone in the city.

The fall of 1961 was very hectic for me. I wrote letters of inquiry, filled out applications, and went to see several dentists for interviews. One day in October, as I was sitting alone in the school cafeteria having lunch, Dr. MacGregor came over and sat down at my table, a mug of coffee in his hand. Up to that time, he had talked to me only a few times briefly in the children's clinic. That day he was in a chatty mood, asking me about China:

whether I knew some previous graduates practising in Hong Kong and about my background and future plans. I was eager to talk with him, because I was interested in an internship, and knew he was the departmental head of children's dentistry at the Hospital for Sick Children. I also knew that he had the reputation of being a crusty old Scot, a very opinionated man with a dominating personality. Several stories had circulated at the school about his shouting match with another professor in the hallway and heated arguments with several students. I was not a witness to these incidents, and actually found him very friendly.

Dr. MacGregor took a good three-quarters of an hour talking to me about my plans, and asked me about doing an internship. I told him that I was very interested, but I also wanted very much to do some travelling first. I had been thinking about joining a group of dentists to attend the World Dental Congress in Cologne, Germany, in the summer of 1962, with an extended excursion to the Middle East. The whole trip was going to take about five weeks. I explained further that, because I had not gone anywhere since my arrival in Toronto as a poor immigrant boy, I really wanted to go on this trip. However, I would need to work a few weeks to make some money first. I then asked him if it was possible for another student to work in my place for the first four months. He advised me that this was problematic, because normally the hospital accepted one dental intern per year for the full twelve months. I was disappointed, because I had thought about someday specializing in dentistry for children. The Hospital for Sick Children was world-famous, and I knew that I could learn a lot. As he got up to leave, he said that he would talk to the admissions committee and see if anything could be done.

About a month later, I was having a difficult session in the clinic with a patient who threw up. Dr. MacGregor came over to my chair and gave me some help in calming the child. He then told me that he had succeeded in arranging everything, and that I could start my internship in August.

My classmate O.C. Hutchinson, a Jamaican, was to do the first three and a half months for me. The salary was not much, at a hundred dollars per month, but a private room was available for me in the residents' quarter. This small room proved to be convenient later, whenever I had to be on call at night – and whenever a girlfriend wanted to visit.

I believed that it took courage for Dr. MacGregor to have chosen the only Asian and black persons in my class of some eighty students, particularly when racial discrimination was still common practice. I was certain that he had had to use considerable efforts on my behalf. He went out on a limb for me. I was determined not to disappoint him.

I also was aware that Dr. MacGregor was involved in many good causes. He raised funds for the Ontario Red Cross and set up a mobile dental clinic on a train, serving remote communities in Northern Ontario where Native Canadians did not have regular dental care. The Red Cross subsequently conferred on him the coveted "Honourary Life Member Award." He was tireless in his effort to help children, particularly those who were disadvantaged. He was the chief architect in setting up departments of dentistry for children at Sick Kids, the Faculty of Dentistry of the University of Toronto, and the Crippled Children's Centre, now known as the Holland Bloorview Kids Rehabilitation Hospital. He would be recognized nationally with a Centennial Medal from the Government of Canada and with an honorary LLD degree from Dalhousie University.

And now, thanks to him, I was about to start an internship. But before that, I had time to work ten weeks in private practice for Dr. James Hing, and earned $2,100, enough for my very memorable journey through Europe and the Middle East. He was another significant mentor in my life.

24

HOPE AND DOUBT

Hope and doubt were powerful emotions that I truly felt deep within me. In the spring of 1962, many of my financial worries, and an inferiority complex, finally began to lift, like yokes taken off an ox after ploughing a rice patty. Freshly armed with a Doctor of Dental Surgery degree, and having secured employment, I was eager to stride forth with some confidence, to reconcile with my past, and to begin a new journey, to be a professional and family man. I felt that the past was beyond my control, best to put it behind me, but the present and future were entirely in my hands, God willing.

On the weekend before my graduation ceremony, I was having lunch at Cousin Joe Jen's home. I liked him, and we talked well into the afternoon. I learned much about his early life in Canada and about my father, who was a younger brother to his dad. Apparently, Father and Dai Ma had sponsored Joe Jen to come to Canada when he was a youth. He said that my father regularly sent remittances to our grandmother in China, and helped many other relatives in need. As we sipped many cups of jasmine tea, he told detailed stories about my family that I hadn't heard before.

BaBa and Dai Ma's generation was certainly much different than mine, one that I had trouble relating to, probably because I was too young and was preoccupied with my own problems rather than trying to understand theirs. They, no doubt, worked extremely hard, doing their very best and achieving a lot for those times and circumstances. My grandfather could only afford to give my father and his brothers a few years of schooling, but my father learned on his own and could write Chinese very well. His English was passable when he spoke, but not when he wrote; for that he depended on Howard and Dorothy. He wanted his children to be educated, able to do well in the mainstream of North American society, an aspiration that was uncommon for the times. Although BaBa and I did not talk very much, more than once he urged me to study hard for a better future. He took me to visit his laundry shop only two or three times, not wanting me to ever have to work there.

The week after my arrival, my father had taken me to the laundry that he and Dai Ma had operated for over twenty years, which was now run by his younger brother and nephews David and Albert. On entering the laundry, I saw a large man with reddish hair and beard talking and gesturing to Third Uncle, who was behind a counter looking for a package among stacks of brown paper parcels lined up on wooden shelves. BaBa said these were clean bundles of laundry for customers, who were paying twenty cents for a shirt and twenty-five cents for a pair of work pants. In the basement, which smelled of soap and soiled laundry, I saw Cousin David pulling wet sheets and pillowcases from monstrous large washing machines and putting them into giant bamboo hampers. In another room, which was uncomfortably hot, we met Cousin Albert hanging up clothing with wooden pegs on parallel clotheslines that ran from one wall to the other. He wiped the sweat from his face before shaking our hands and complaining about the heat.

I didn't like the look and smell of the laundry, and visiting it once or twice more over the following two years only increased this distaste. The work was honourable labour, and somebody had to do it, to keep people clean, healthy, and looking fine on Sundays, but, for me, it was too mind-numbing. I promised myself that I would study, so I would never have to work there. Luckily, I never did, unlike my older siblings, who grew up in the same building and had to help with the ironing, packaging, customer service, and other chores after school. For that, I thank my lucky stars, BaBa and Dai Ma.

When my father was stricken with cancer, he had written his own will in Chinese, with messages for us children. At the reading of his will, I was somewhat apprehensive that I might be relegated to the status of a second-class son again. The will was read, and I was treated equally with my siblings. I recognized then that I had been too immature, judgemental, and narrow-minded to appreciate him. Sadly, I realized that I had always harboured a quiet resentment in my heart, feeling like a lesser son who had been abandoned, and that I had never expressed to him my gratitude or love.

My father's desire to retire to Canton and live in his dream home never came to fruition. He lived long enough to see me, but regrettably not my mother. I had often wondered if his spirit was happy and at peace, never having returned to visit my mother and his beloved homeland.

Later, kneeling at his grave, I suddenly remembered a quotation in *The Prophet*, a book by Kahlil Gibran that I was reading, which goes something like this: "A philosopher said to a street sweeper, 'I pity you. Yours is a hard and dirty task.' And the street sweeper replied, 'Thank you, Sir. But tell me what your work is?' And the philosopher answered, 'I study man's mind and his deeds.' Then the street sweeper went on with his work, and said with a smile, 'I pity you too.'"

I slowly traced my fingers along his name and I whispered, "BaBa, I looked down on your work; I realize that there is no shame in honest toil.

You did your best and provided well for all of us. I judged you without really knowing you and the circumstances you faced. Forgive me, BaBa. Thank you." However, I still couldn't say, "BaBa, I love you."

Shifting over to Dai Ma's side, I also traced my finger in the characters of her name, Lee Hees. I remembered writing her Chinese name with a big brush on a sheet of rice paper for the stone artisan to carve onto the granite. My sister had requested that I should write it, instead of using a professional Chinese calligrapher, even though I told her that my calligraphy was very amateurish. Looking at my not-so-elegant handiwork, I whispered: "Dai Ma, you were a good person. Thank you for taking care of me for six years. Forgive me for the troubles that I caused you. Now I know better and can appreciate you more."

I quietly added, "BaBa, Dai Ma, I'll try to visit more; your graves will not be neglected; I'll tell my future children to honour you. I am now a Canadian citizen and I will settle permanently in this country and bring you flowers. I now have a job as a dentist and I am saving money. Don't worry about me; I'll be fine." I stood up and bowed deeply to my father and to Dai Ma three times each. I walked away with my head high, feeling cleansed.

The next day was graduation day, May 28, 1962. I joined my classmates in the foyer of University College, dressed in black ceremonial regalia. I was called to line up behind Joe Girdlestone in the leading group of dental graduates, those who had graduated summa cum laude. We walked proudly and briskly across the campus, and entered the amphitheatre-like Convocation Hall. After listening to speeches, we were called one by one to be presented to the chancellor of the university, after which we received our degrees of Doctor of Dental Surgery.

Emerging onto the campus lawn, I was surrounded by well-wishers. The *Toronto Daily Star* interviewed me briefly and reported the next day: "The largest gallery of relatives at the ceremonies came to watch Chinese-born Alan Joe, 24, of Ontario Street, receive his doctorate of dental surgery." The *Globe and Mail* printed a photo of me with my Cousin Che King from Hong Kong, who was travelling on a world tour and had stopped in Toronto for three days. Gathered around me were my mother, Cousin Che King, my brother, sister, their spouses and children, and Uncle Lowe Joe and his family, a total of sixteen persons. They had taken a Monday off work or school to attend my graduation. I was profoundly moved and felt that day's sunshine was unusually warm.

That evening my sister hosted a party at her home in my honour; there was plenty of food and a huge cake. In addition to our family, nine other persons were invited. My mother wore a new dress that day and was beaming every time I looked her way. I felt happy for her, because this was validation for her as much as it was for me. She had endured and sacrificed so much, and frequently reminded me: "Your education is the most important means to your future, to be somebody. You're lucky to be in Canada, where nearly all things are possible."

In that spring of 1962, I felt that the years of hardship, doubt, and perseverance had finally brought me close to the realization of my dreams: I had made peace with Father and Dai Ma; my siblings had honoured and accepted me as an equal; I was already practising dentistry, which I loved, and making a good living. I had signed on for travels to Europe and the Middle East, and to start working at the Hospital for Sick Children upon my return. I had begun to think of other opportunities that were available, such as post-graduate studies.

Professor McGregor had hinted that he might have a position for me later, teaching children's dentistry at the Faculty. Time for romance too, I thought, as I smiled at my good fortune.

25

GREAT EXPECTATIONS

With great expectations, I began my dental residency at the Hospital for Sick Children in the summer of 1962. One major goal was to learn more about treatments for children, particularly those with mental and/or physical challenges. Another was to look for some fun and romance, which I had never had much time for up to that point. On previous visits to the hospital, I had noticed that the place was full of young, gorgeous-looking nurses. Being single and unattached at the time, I was looking forward to having a really good time there.

In early September, I was invited to a house party in Rosedale by Maura, an Irish nurse at the hospital. At the party, I met a nurse of Japanese descent. She was very attractive and vivacious. I danced with her many times that evening and subsequently we would go out on more dates, one of which was on the occasion of the University of Toronto's Chinese Overseas Students Dance, on November 16. Hailey looked dainty, like a five-foot-tall doll, full of energy, and she could really dance too.

During a break for refreshments that same evening, my friends Louise and Fred Mark introduced me to a friend of theirs, an operating-room nurse named Juliana Jean Shee. Louise called her by her middle name, Jean. For the entire evening, I danced only with my date. However, when Hailey went to the powder room, I watched Jean dancing with Fred. I noticed that she had excellent posture and great-looking legs. My eyes lit up, but I did not have an opportunity to talk to her again that evening. I had a chore to do as the Master of Ceremonies for that evening's program, aside from having fun dancing with my date.

One day early in December, I met Juliana Jean in the corridor at the hospital. We started a conversation, and I invited her to the staff Christmas party on December 19. At the end of that evening, I made another date with her for early in the New Year. We went out for dinner on January 4, 1963. We talked very candidly about our lives and our travels. I found her enchanting. Her smile, frankness, and appealing British accent captivated me.

Apparently, before coming to Canada, she had gone to England from Hong Kong to study nursing for five years. She was refreshingly different, and did not play coy like some of the girls that I had previously met. I was smitten. A week later we had dinner again; this time it was at my apartment, together with several of my old friends from high school. On our fourth date, she asked me to call her Jean, the name her family had given her. She chose the name Juliana when she converted to Roman Catholicism. She cooked a very fine dinner of pork chops at her place, and we went to see the movie *Mutiny on the Bounty*. Over my protests, she bought the tickets. I discovered some time later that it was her birthday, January 18.

Over the next few months, Juliana Jean and I saw each other frequently at the hospital, and we went out once or twice a week. I got to know her better. She was the youngest of five children, with two older brothers and two sisters. She had lost both of her parents; her mother had died from post-childbirth complications when giving birth to a younger sibling, who unfortunately did not survive. Antibiotics had not been developed at that time. Jean was only two years old, and was cared for mainly by a very devoted amah, or "nanny," and her mother's younger sisters. Her father, who had graduated in Chemistry from Columbia University in New York, had remarried and gone to Taiwan to teach English to medical students. He had passed away in Taiwan in 1961.

For some years Jean lived with her mother's younger sister, Auntie Fanny, and her husband, Uncle Edmund, in Hong Kong. They raised her like their own daughter. She attended Maryknoll Convent School in Kowloon, Hong Kong. To pursue her career, she went to study nursing at the Royal Surrey County Hospital in Guildford, England. She then moved to London to study midwifery at St. Thomas' Hospital. She did not have a car and could not ride a bicycle, so delivering babies was problematic. Also, she didn't like delivering babies in the middle of the night. She changed her program and went to Brompton Chest Hospital to become an operating-room nurse, specializing in heart and thoracic surgery. She immigrated to Canada in 1961, working briefly at Toronto East General Hospital, and then had come over to the Hospital for Sick Children, where I happened to work.

During our courtship, we walked and used public transportation. Fortunately, Jean did not mind at all, as she knew that I was not making much money. Even in February, the snow and sleet did not deter us. Waiting at the stops or walking arm in arm for many blocks was a little disconcerting, but it gave us opportunities to cuddle. We walked the streets when the weather was fine and enjoyed looking at the architecture and people.

She was dainty and delicate, yet I found that she moved about with an air of certainty that suggested a strong will and a quick temper. Things were not always smooth, as we did have a few disagreements. Nevertheless, I was very much in love with her. She was beautiful, very smart, had a good heart, and was so sweet – most of the time.

By the summer of 1963, Juliana Jean had met my mother several times and they seemed to like each other. She decided that the July 1 long weekend would be a good time for us to go to New York City, to visit some of her closest relatives in America, her mother's sisters. I met Aunt Fanny and Aunt Katie and their husbands Uncle Ed and Uncle Ling, respectively. Her relatives welcomed me warmly and treated me with great hospitality. I had the impression they liked me.

Our love blossomed. We thought we were ready to settle down, because we had both enjoyed some years of bachelorhood, and had also travelled extensively to different parts of the world. I began to think about how best to propose to her.

July 21, 1963, was my twenty-sixth birthday. The day was glorious, with sunshine and a gentle breeze. Juliana Jean and I went to High Park, and wandered through the park and the rock garden to a small lake called Grenadier Pond. As a teenager, I had lived not too far from this pond and had fished there for perch, sunfish, and bass. I rented a boat and we rowed leisurely on the pristine water. Under the shadows of majestic oaks and maples, we floated and listened to music from a band playing nearby. When I thought the moment was perfect, I handed my beloved a letter that I had carefully written the previous day. In it, I told her briefly my life story, my aspirations, and my admiration and profound love for her. The last sentence was "Will you be my wife?"

I waited anxiously as she read. She came into my arms and kissed me ardently. We kissed some more after she said "Yes." The boat rocked precariously, and then it drifted gently towards shore.

To love and be loved is an exhilarating experience. In mid-October Juliana Jean and I booked a week off and took the bus north to Huntsville to see the autumn foliage. We stayed at Divine Lake Lodge on Mary Lake. The main lodge and several small cottages were set in a picturesque clearing in the silent woods. We were the only guests there, and the owners treated us with utmost hospitality and excellent food.

During the day, we walked for miles along paths and narrow roads canopied with magnificent maples and pines, our feet cushioned by brown needles and red leaves. The crimson forests and the blue jays were in their full glory. For a couple of evenings, we donned sweaters and sat on the dock, admiring the stars while the aroma of cedar surrounded us. In the quiet of the night we could hear water lapping against the rocks, and were sometimes startled by the wistful call of the loons.

In the fall of 1963 we began planning our wedding in earnest for the following spring. After consulting the Chinese zodiac, we chose the auspicious day of Saturday, April 11, 1964.

We made reservations for a Chinese banquet at the Golden Dragon Restaurant. The church was to be Saint Basil's, where Juliana Jean frequently attended mass. She had wanted a small wedding, while I had wanted a bigger one of at least 200 people, because of my many relatives and friends in Toronto. We finally settled on 190 guests, about average for the Chinese.

During our engagement, I asked Juliana Jean if she would agree to have my mother live with us after we were married. My mother and I enjoyed a very strong bond. To my relief, Juliana Jean understood my feelings. She was very gracious and readily agreed.

Our wedding on April 11, 1964, finally arrived. For early spring in Toronto, it was surprisingly warm and sunny with a breeze. Philip Jew, my best man, drove me in a rented Cadillac to Saint Basil's Catholic Church. Father Purdue, a jolly Dominican priest, greeted us warmly. He had previously given me instruction on Roman Catholicism and was always kind and patient with me.

Our bridal party consisted of three junior bridesmaids: Jackie Mark, Susan Joe, and Lucinda Wong. Jackie's brother Douglas Mark was our page boy, with Holly Yip as our flower girl. Senior bridesmaid was Janet Joe, and the maid of honour was Margaret Lai. Helping me were groomsmen Bill Sinclair, Karl Karson, Clifford Lee, and Gilbert Chu.

The ceremony started at one o'clock, with the organist playing Handel's *Water Music*, chosen by my bride. She looked radiant and exquisite in her Empire Line white wedding dress, headpiece, and veil, as she walked towards me on the arm of her favourite uncle, Ed. Father Purdue officiated.

After a photo session outside the church in brilliant sunshine, we newlyweds and our immediate family went back to our home for the traditional Chinese tea ceremony. The bride was to bow and to serve a cup of tea with both hands to each elder member of the groom's family. My mother had the honour of receiving the first cup. Mother took a sip; she then gave my bride gifts of gold and jade jewellery, as was the Chinese custom.

Soon it was five o'clock, time to go to our reception at six. We had reserved nineteen tables. On each table, we placed a bottle of Johnny Walker scotch, as well as wines for our non-Chinese guests. The banquet was a nine-course dinner, which included roasted pig, bird's-nest soup, braised abalone and duck, steamed black Chinese mushrooms, crispy chicken, steamed fish, snow peas and vegetables, fried rice and noodles. Dessert was a sweet liquid made with lotus seeds. It was a memorable celebration among family and friends.

Feeling that I had found the love of my life to share the future, I could hardly believe my good fortune when I looked back at the struggle and often the frightening uncertainties of those early years. I began to understand that life's great sorrows and challenges could also bestow a unique insight into human existence. Could I have appreciated life's sweet moments as deeply without the hurts? It was Kahlil Gibran who said that Beauty is found in both a tear and a smile combined. "Beauty is that harmony between joy and sorrow which begins within our holy of holies and ends beyond the scope of our imagination." Most significant to me now were the feelings of peace, hope, and reconciliation – the stuff my dreams were made of. It was Eleanor Roosevelt who said: "The future belongs to those who believe in the beauty of their dreams." And Gibran in *The Prophet* wrote:

Only when you drink from the river of silence, shall you indeed sing.

And when you have reached the mountain top, then shall you begin to climb.

And when the earth shall claim your limbs, then shall you truly dance.

Was I ready to start climbing the mountain, to see what was on top and beyond the clouds? With renewed confidence, I began to dream and hope.

Immigration document of my father, Chow Wa-yoi (aka Yue Joe), 1912

Nine-year-old Alan Joe in Canton (Guangzhou)

My brother's wedding, 1949
Left to right: my sister, Dorothy, Howard and Hazel, my father, Dai Ma

My graduation picture,
University of Toronto, Doctor of
Dental Surgery, 1962

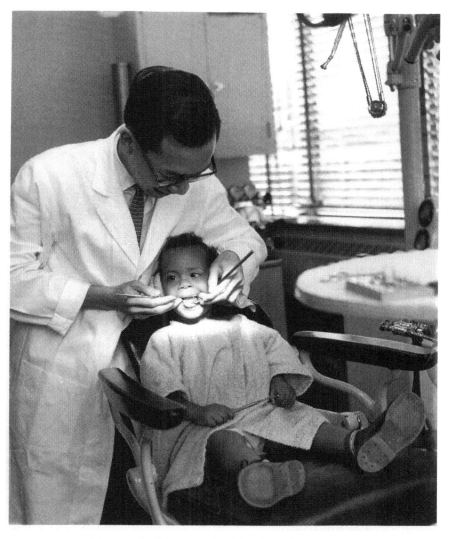

Working at the Toronto Children's Aid Society, 1962

Our wedding party, St. Basil's Roman Catholic Church,
Toronto, April 11, 1964

Our wedding, left to right: Ruth Lin (bride's aunt), my mother,
Janet Joe (my cousin), Margaret Lai (bride's cousin), the bride
and groom, Fanny and Edmund Lew (bride's aunt and uncle)

Mark and Petina

Receiving a fellowship from the International College of Dentists, 1993

My family, taken for my mother's 80th birthday, 1989
Left to right, rear: me, Petina, and Mark
Left to right, front: my mother and Juliana Jean

My mother's 90th birthday, 1999. In the front row, between Juliana Jean and my mother (centre), is my sister, Dorothy (in front of her husband, Ed). Behind Petina and me are my brother, Howard, and his second wife, Barbara. Mark is in the rear at the right.

WORK, LOVE, PLAY – AND SPIRITUALITY

What Came After

26

HOME, SCHOOL, AND WORK

Marriage means love, stability, but also responsibility to more than oneself, and the desire to build a home and have children. Our life together was good and full of promise, although we had a few problems, because on a few occasions my wife, my mother, and I got into some conflicts. This situation was inevitable when a mother-in-law and daughter-in-law live in the same home, and each person has different life experiences and expectations. The generational and cultural gaps were very hard to bridge at times, and I was caught in the middle. I really did not know what to do as I tried to please both parties. I was a dutiful son brought up in the Chinese tradition, and, having shared very hard times, my mother and I had a very strong bond, even though we were separated throughout my teenage years. I could not bear to abandon her to live alone, but what would Juliana Jean think about this matter?

She did try very hard to accommodate my mother's old-fashioned ways; still, Juliana Jean was often annoyed. We all suffered. At such times I was very distressed, because I loved both women. I didn't know how to explain to my mother the ways of a modern marriage, how she needed to change her attitudes and adapt to a daughter-in-law a generation younger. I was afraid of hurting her feelings too much, although she was a stoic person and seldom complained. It was my fault for not setting out what was expected of each woman when we first got married. Traditional Chinese families with two, three, or more generations living under one roof were getting less common as China became westernized. (We would manage to live together in the same home for seventeen years, but eventually, I decided that we would all be happier if my mother lived independently. I bought her a condominium, just across the street from my clinic. During the week, I would walk over to her place for lunch, and then take a little nap before returning to work. The whole family would have dinner at Grandma's every Sunday. This arrangement worked out satisfactorily.)

With my mother helping to take care of our first child, baby Mark, Juliana Jean went back to work at Sunnybrook Hospital, part-time. Her income helped us save more each month, because I was thinking of going back to university, to be a specialist. I had enjoyed my internship working with children, so naturally, I thought about that specialty.

After the completion of my internship, I began to work at three places: The Hospital for Sick Children, the dental clinic at Metropolitan Toronto Children's Aid Society on Charles Street, and a clinic uptown at Yonge and Lawrence, with Dr. Morley Crockford. He was one of my former clinical instructors, and recruited me to work as his associate when I was in my graduating year. At his very busy clinic, I worked mostly on children: fillings, root canals, extractions, preventive dentistry, and other procedures. In three years, I did only one set of full dentures, for an elderly lady, and it was quite an experience, as I needed to do several adjustments to make them fit well. I was happy I didn't have any more patients who needed full dentures, because I don't think I was very good at it.

In doing family dentistry, I found it difficult to switch from one task to another all day long; each task required different skills and instruments. On top of that, a dentist had to deal with all kinds of characters – and with those who may have phobias about dentists. We often hurt our patients inadvertently while performing unpleasant procedures such as root canals; we also hurt their pocketbooks. Many people harbour the notion that dentists charge too much, not realizing that the overhead expenses for most dental offices run very high, at approximately 60 per cent of income, or more.

At the Children's Aid Society, I tried to do a lot of preventive dentistry, which included cleaning and the application of topical fluoride to strengthen the teeth against cavities. At that time, dental decay was rampant, because fluoride was not yet used in Toronto's municipal drinking water. Politicians and public figures like Gordon Sinclair objected to putting fluoride in the drinking water, calling it a rat poison. Every day I did a lot of pulling and filling of rotten teeth, even for some three- and four-year-olds. Many of those children came from broken homes, and they might not even have had decent toothbrushes, let alone dental floss. A few of them were very tough and rough kids, who swore like longshoremen. One teenager said to me just as I was preparing to work on his dark-grey front teeth, "Hey, Doc, you ain't gonna jab me with that f—ing needle!" It was no mean accomplishment finishing the root-canal treatments on his two front incisors.

By the fall of 1965, Juliana Jean and I felt that we had accumulated enough savings for me to return to university. I was interested in specializing in either children's dentistry or orthodontics. Feeling that treating young children with challenges was much more taxing than adolescents and teenagers, I decided I wanted to be an orthodontist.

I applied in the fall of 1965 to the University of Toronto, the only institution in Ontario at that time with a specialty program in orthodontics.

Each year the competition among approximately one hundred applicants was furious for the six spots available. I thought my chances were a little better than fifty-fifty, since I had graduated with first-class honours, ranking eighth in a class of some eighty students. Also in my favour was a year of experience interning at the Hospital for Sick Children.

Anxiously I waited to hear from the university. Finally, one morning in January 1966, my wife handed me a letter from the university. With eager anticipation, I tore open the envelope. Juliana Jean hugged me tightly without a word when she saw my grim expression. I told her I had not made it: I felt dejected and humbled. She comforted me after reading the letter, saying that I still had a chance, since the notice said I was the first alternate. I could also try again the following year. Meanwhile both of us could work an extra year to save more money for the twenty-four months needed for the program, which would be a benefit, as we now had a new baby to care for.

Then, one day in April 1966, Professor Painter called to tell me that Joe Girdlestone, the gold medallist of my class of 1962, had withdrawn because of illness, and it was my call if I wanted to take his place. I was very happy to accept the invitation.

In June 1966, I began the first month of our two-year program. That summer we spent most of our time acquiring technical skills in bending and soldering wires, fitting bands, and constructing orthodontic plates. I was not gifted with technical skills like my fellow student Eric Luks, nor did I have the scientific mind of Bill Sinclair or the general excellence of Ray Bozek. Roland Albert and Bryan Smith were also superb students. I had to work extremely hard to keep up with my classmates. My fingers became raw and bleeding with blisters from bending so many wires.

It was terribly hot that summer, and that little lab that we worked in was not air-conditioned. It was literally a sweatshop, with unbearable working conditions. In addition, Ed, the chief technician who supervised us, was giving me a lot of aggravation. Both the departments of orthodontics and prosthodontics relied heavily on him to manage the technique courses, so he had enormous power and influence in the faculty. He was excellent technically, but his personality was the opposite. He loved to embarrass students, particularly quiet and stoic persons like myself. I often found that I had passed some procedures by my academic instructors, but was still not good enough to please him. He made me do them all over again. He was a miser when giving us materials for our technique courses – so much so that, on a couple of occasions, I ran to a dental company to buy the necessary stuff myself, instead of asking him.

One day, Ed was particularly obnoxious to me about some technical stuff. I blew up and told him to get off my back. I muttered under my breath, "Go to hell," as I stormed out of his office. I was expecting the worst, but nothing happened; there was not a word from my departmental head, Dr. Woodside.

The heavy academic subjects of anatomy, radiology, and genetics began in earnest in September, right after Labour Day. Again, I struggled to keep up with my classmates, led by Ray Bozek, a top graduate of the 1963 class. To earn extra money, I worked as a general dentist on Saturdays, at Dr. Horst Vogel's clinic. It made my weekends rather short, with not enough time for rest and recreation. I regretted that I did not have much energy left for quality time with my family, particularly my young son. I had to quit working on Saturdays after some eight months, because I fell asleep too often at my desk.

The last six months of my graduate program were extremely hectic and stressful. At school, I needed to write my thesis, finish my cases on time, type up reports, and study for final exams. At home, we were expecting our second child that April, and our apartment lease was expiring a month before the new arrival. We had to find another accommodation, because our landlord had a relative who wanted our apartment. That spring I was also busy looking for an office location so I could set up my practice as soon as possible after graduation. I looked at all the districts in Greater Toronto and found three possible areas: Don Mills, Richmond Hill, and West Toronto.

I went to visit each area several times, and talked to the family dentists, orthodontists, and pharmacists to find out what opportunities there were to locate my practice. I finally decided on Weston, a suburb in West Toronto, because it could accommodate a new orthodontist. One of my teachers, Dr. Gunnar Lie, had a clinic on Royal York Road, and he was kind enough to invite me to his area.

Even on Sunday evenings, I needed to read books and journals in preparation for Mondays. I was exhausted much of the time, but I survived. I must give credit and express my gratitude to my wife for her loving care and encouragement, in addition to keeping the children quiet. She worked part time and helped me with typing.

Fortunately, I was able to finish active treatment for nearly all my assigned patients on time to graduate in June, and I did well enough that I was welcomed back to teach orthodontics twice a week, to third- and fourth-year dental students. As our savings were nearly depleted, I was happy to receive a small salary from the univerity. Meanwhile I needed to find a location to build a practice.

After some weeks of careful searching in the spring of 1968, I found a good location on Kipling Avenue in a suburb in West Toronto. The space was only a little over eight hundred square feet, rather small for a clinic, but the landlord was helpful and willing to install plumbing, power and partially decorate the place to my specifications. I thought the rent was reasonable at $225 a month for the first two years and then $300 for the next three years. I signed the lease with an option for three more years.

Before my graduation, Juliana Jean ran around looking for a place for us to live, hopefully not too far from my future clinic. Finally, she found a large townhouse on Sedgeley Drive. Our new home had two stories, a fully finished basement, two washrooms (this was a luxury for us!) and three bedrooms, one of which we needed as a nursery for our new baby. We moved into this rental house at the end of March 1968.

Petina Clare, our second child, was born on April 20, 1968, two months before I was due to graduate. It was a hectic time, with deadlines for numerous things to be done. Nevertheless, Petina was a great joy to us, as now we had a boy and a girl. Mark never displayed any jealousy and was very loving to his little sister.

During this time, I visited three different banks, and eventually borrowed $15,000 from the Imperial Bank on Elizabeth Street in old Chinatown. With this loan, I bought two dental chairs and some equipment from Chicago. Mr. Walker, the bank manager, gave me very favourable rates and terms of repayment. It was helpful that I knew him from when I was working at Lichee Garden, where he often came for lunch. My clinic opened on the auspicious day of August 16, according to the Chinese almanac, which listed good and bad days to do certain activities.

Everything was coming together nicely by the fall. I was getting two or three new patients every week, and the dentists in my area were very supportive, particularly Drs. Art Tarshis, Ron Anco, Donald Chiang, Irwin Rose, and my classmate Mike Johnston. Juliana Jean was helping me as my receptionist and dental assistant, because I could ill afford to hire anyone.

However, life can take an unlucky turn. Late on the snowy evening of November 17, 1968, we had a terrible accident with my first car, a Chrysler Valiant, bought for $2,400 in November 1963. A big Pontiac driven by a teenager lost control on the slippery road, slid across the median, and smashed into the front of our car. Juliana Jean's left ankle was shattered and needed extensive surgery. I sustained cuts to my lips and chin, and my lower teeth were knocked loose. I hurt for three months before I recovered fully. My wife took much longer because of the severity of her injuries.

I urgently required help at home, because my mother could not manage by herself, so our friend Rose Lee came often to help with our baby. My wife's nephew Andrew Shee, who was living with us while attending Martingrove Collegiate, also helped at changing of diapers and other chores. At the office, Professor George Hare's wife, Ann, a good friend, came to my aid and served as my receptionist for nearly two weeks, until I found a new assistant in Linda Gillis, a retired air hostess. She was very good at public relations and a fine assistant.

Time was rough for our little family for nearly two years, because Juliana Jean was in and out of the hospital with pain in her foot and back. She walked with crutches and felt miserable that she could not care personally for her baby. However, in that time, she did a magnificent job in accomplishing many other things for me and the family. When we decided to move, she looked around and found a delightful two-storey home on La Rose Avenue. It was a small house with about 750 square feet on each floor, but it was a cosy home and we had a luxury I never had before, three washrooms!

By the fifth year of our marriage, we were happily settled in our lovely little home, only six or seven minutes' drive from my office. Our children, Mark and Petina, were delightful, well adjusted, and a constant joy to us. Indeed, we were blessed.

27

A PROFESSIONAL REGRET

The Chinese have an old saying, "Go up the mountain too often, you will encounter the tiger." Doctors see many patients a day, over two hundred days a year. Mistakes are bound to happen. While I am an orthodontist and not a physician, I have treated many thousands of patients over a career of nearly forty years. To my deep regret, I did make one notable professional mistake, and I literally paid for it.

In the 1980s, I had a patient called Lily (not her real name). She was a very pretty eleven-year-old, but her smile was disfigured. Her upper eye teeth stuck out like the fangs of Dracula, and her front teeth were extremely crooked. She was referred to me for orthodontic treatment by Dr. K, her family dentist. I examined Lily's teeth and found that most of her teeth were adult or permanent teeth, except for a couple of baby teeth that were still present. Subsequently, I sent a letter to Dr. K, saying that Lily's teeth were very crowded. I strongly recommended the extraction of four adult premolars, to gain the spaces necessary to straighten her teeth. I also asked Dr. K to send me a full set of her X-rays, so that I could decide on a definitive treatment plan.

Some weeks later, Lily came back to my office, and I saw that she had already had four permanent teeth extracted. I looked for her X-rays, but did not find any. My nurse called Dr. K's office, and three days later we received her X-rays. I examined the films and, to my horror, I discovered that Lily was born missing one permanent premolar, called tooth #45. That meant she should have had three premolars extracted instead of four. This was clearly an error. The fault was partly mine, because I had recommended the four extractions, and partly Dr. K's, because he had gone ahead and pulled the teeth without either checking the X-rays carefully or alerting me about the congenitally missing tooth. The next day I met with Dr. K. We agonized over what to do, fearful of a malpractice lawsuit and the tarnishing of our reputations.

Finally, I decided to meet with the patient and her parents. I told them exactly what had happened and that Lily would later require an implant to supply the fourth premolar tooth. I apologized and expressed my deep regrets. I further advised them to consult their family lawyer. They were visibly upset, but I didn't see any anger.

A few weeks later, I met with the family again. They asked for $10,000 as compensation. I immediately phoned Dr. K and he agreed to pay half of it. We felt that settling this way was better and far less stressful for everyone, amicably and out of court. Subsequently, I paid my share of $5,000, and legal papers were signed. Eventually, I did straighten Lily's teeth, and because the implant was located near the back of the mouth, her lovely smile was not affected.

It was a valuable and costly lesson, but I learned that integrity and professionalism is the best policy. Most people are fair-minded if they are treated with sincerity and respect. Since then, I don't believe I have made any more such major mistakes. When I was teaching, I always reminded my orthodontic students to check X-rays carefully, write their correspondence precisely, count the teeth, and treat people with respect. I realized that I had made a mistake and paid the price, but was consoled by another Chinese proverb, "Admit error, change, and be wise."

28

FAREWELL TO MOTHER

The oxygen machine hissed incessantly as I watched Mother's chest rise and fall ever so imperceptibly. I had sat for several hours in Room 210 of the palliative-care ward of Scarborough Grace Hospital. Mother had not awakened for two full days, and most of that time I remained by her bedside and reflected on our life together. I began to write something on a notepad, my eulogy to her:

Dear Family and Friends. This indeed is a sad time but please do not grieve! We are here to celebrate a long and productive life. Mother was born in 1909, at the time of great upheavals in China, when the old Manchu Dynasty was crumbling and revolutionary armies of different stripes and ideologies fought for dominance to set up the first republic in China. Chaos and starvation were rampant throughout the whole country, and my mother's family, being poor, had suffered more than most. My mother embodied the fate of traditional Chinese girls, who were silenced at birth because of their gender. Not only was she deprived of a formal education, my mother was given away when she was nine years old.

Mother was always reluctant to tell me much about her childhood, saying that she had nothing worthwhile to tell me. I learned or guessed that her father had died when she was very young, and a family, in a town called Kong Moon, had adopted her. There she did most of the household chores, like a maid more than a daughter. When she was nineteen, a marriage to my father was arranged, so that she had a home and a "rice bowl." A year later a son was born, but tragically he died at age two. At age twenty-eight, Mother gave birth to another son: me. It was 1937, and war had just broken out between China and Japan. My father had to leave us behind in Guangzhou, as he left for Canada to escape the war. My mother and I did not have visas for Canada, and thus we suffered the years of enemy occupation.

The war years were horrific for Mother and me. To escape Japanese bombings and their advancing armies, we had to flee to many places, eventually to settle in our ancestor's village in the country. In Nam Bin, we found an empty old house without any furniture, running water, or electricity. There was also no land for us to farm for a living. When a few months later we came under direct Japanese occupation and postal service from North America was cut, we could not receive any remittances from my father. Our situation was desperate, with starvation staring at us. Mother worked as a peddler, selling such things as salted fish and tofu, from dawn to dusk. I was left all alone with an occasional look-in from a neighbour's young wife. I was hungry a lot of the time; my mother and I were often sick, but she kept working to keep us alive.

We survived those years from 1942 to 1945, when World War II came to an end. Immediately, we went back to our hometown of Guangzhou, where we found our family home mostly destroyed: no furniture, no toilets, nothing except a skeleton of a house. My mother had to rebuild everything. Fortunately, by then, my father was able to send us money.

We had hardly settled into a reasonably normal life when civil war erupted between the Nationalists and Communists. Mao Zedong was winning, and by 1949, we had to flee our home again and go to the British colony of Hong Kong. Two months later, I left Hong Kong with my Uncle Number Four and travelled to Canada. My mother remained behind. We were separated for seven years, and it was not until 1957 that I was able to arrange for her to join me in Toronto. By then, my father had been dead for six years.

When my mother arrived in Toronto, I was in my first year at the University of Toronto. Financially, I was strapped, so my mother again had to go to work on a farm to support us until I became a dentist. Throughout all the years of war and peace, trials and tribulations, births and deaths, Mother remained optimistic and was always there for me. Very rarely did she complain. Fortunately, the last forty years of her life were pretty good ones for her: she enjoyed relatively good health and her grandchildren, Mark and Petina, were her pride and joy.

Mother was one of the wisest individuals I have ever known. She was a spiritual person, although she did not regularly attend any temple or church. She taught me about love and compassion: to be lovingly kind to all living creatures, as we share our existence with all that live in this universe. Without a father present, I learned nearly everything from her.

She also taught me about peace. When I was attending Christian missionary school in China, we sometimes attended service at a Baptist church. One of our favourite hymns in Cantonese was St. Francis of Assisi's "Lord, make me a channel of your peace. / Where there is hatred, let me sow love. Where there is injury, pardon." Mother was always gentle, dignified, and conciliatory. She told me numerous times: "There is no shame in being poor, as long as you have dignity, integrity, and compassion." She lived by this code of ethics all her life, and I have tried to never forget it.

She taught me not to lie. Once as a child I told her a lie. She spanked me on the legs with a bamboo stick. I cried for a few minutes, with more noise than pain, but she wept for hours. She was broken-hearted about her own perceived failure to teach me right from wrong. I remember that lesson well.

Mother taught me to be a good listener. Whenever she thought I was listening poorly to her she would say, "Are you listening to me with your ears or with your teeth?"

I would reply, "I can hear you pretty well with my teeth. Don't you think my teeth look pretty good for hearing?" I would then flash her a big smile. She would call me a little idiot.

She constantly encouraged me to study and learn new things, whatever the subject matter. To this day, every fall and winter, I enrol in some educational courses, ranging from auto mechanics to poetry.

Yes, my mother did not attend any formal school, while I have had many teachers and professors with multiple degrees. Yet she was my best teacher. I shall miss her. I shall miss my weekly lunches with her!

This eulogy was delivered on the sunny afternoon of August 28, 2002, in the chapel of the Humphrey Funeral Home. That day I experienced a wide spectrum of feelings: sadness, bereavement, a sense of closure, relief, and fulfillment. I had fulfilled my promise to my father when he was dying, that I would take care of my mother and myself.

An era had ended. My guiding light for nearly seventy years had now been extinguished. However, her spirit will always be with me. A few days before my mother's passing, I wrote a poem in her honour:

Farewell, Dear Mother, Por
You gave me life and lessons galore,
So much love, devotion, and peace.
On your back, we crossed mountains and seas
You shielded me from bombs and grenades,
In wars with Japanese and Red Brigades.
The Pearl River runs fast and deep,
You have sailed thousands of miles and earned your sleep.
Angels have come to sing you lullabies,
Peace, Mother, farewell and goodbye.

29

REAP THE HARVEST

My work has been likened to sowing seeds. I have been inspired by the words of a favourite philosopher, Kahlil Gibran. He said in part, "work is to sow seeds with tenderness and reap the harvest with joy, even as if your beloved were to eat the fruit. It is to charge all things you fashion with a breath of your spirit."

Throughout my career, I have loved my work. At the end of orthodontic treatment for patients, I derived great satisfaction in seeing their big smiles. They looked happy and confident, with healthy and straight teeth. I also feel it is important to be a positive human being, particularly with young people, who made up the vast majority of my clientele. When a boy or girl came to me for orthodontics, it normally meant that I would see him or her monthly for approximately two years, then semi-annually for checkups for three more years. These are important years and represent a significant portion of their young lives. It was beneficial to them as well as to me for us to be friends, particularly if they had problems at home or school. Whenever appropriate, I counselled young people on diet and nutrition, schooling and smoking. They might listen to me a little more than their parents, particularly when they had very little choice while sitting in my chair!

Now that I have retired, I sometime think back to the many excellent patients who inspired me to work harder. In the spring of 2004, a former patient whom I helped more than ten years before came to visit me. J and his sister had been in active treatment with me when their mother fell ill with a serious illness. She had to quit her job, and money became a concern. I tried my best to comfort them and reduced my fees, so the children could continue their treatment to completion. J talked about his family, and his present studies in dentistry in the United States. He discussed with me his plans to do graduate studies in orthodontics, and his desire to return to Ontario to practise and teach. As he smiled, I sneaked a few glances at his mouth, and was gratified to see that his teeth still looked good. He said I was his role model, and thanked me for my kindness and inspiration. Actually, we inspired each other. He reminded me a lot of myself when I was his age.

As J drove off on his way back to Case Western University in Cleveland, I was filled with a feeling of pride. A few years later, I learned that he did become an orthodontist. I believe that with fine young people like him my profession and the public will be well served. I like to think that I may have made a difference in the lives of a number of young people, that my aspiration to sow seeds has yielded some harvest.

Timing is everything. It is no less true to know the right time to retire. My career in private practice and teaching had been a huge blessing, because it suited me so well. Throughout, I worked diligently with love and pride, constantly learning to keep up with new developments in my field. When I approached the age of sixty, my accountant told me that my wife and I should be able to retire comfortably. I began to plan for retirement, and think about what hobbies or interests I should pursue afterwards.

Finding a successor to take good care of my patients and employees, and not leaving things to chance or the last minute, was very important to me. I still found my work fulfilling and enjoyed learning new ways to treat orthodontic problems. However, successful retirement and the smooth transition in a practice required careful planning. For over two years, I attended lectures and seminars on this subject.

I started looking for candidates who would eventually take over the practice that I had built since 1968. My son, Mark, was happy practising family dentistry in another office. He had worked part-time in my clinic, and I had taught him a lot about orthodontics, but he was not prepared to go back to school for three more years to specialize. I interviewed about a dozen candidates who had graduated from either an American university, the University of Toronto, or the University of Western Ontario. They came to the office and met my staff. I valued the opinions of my staff in selecting a young colleague who might someday be their boss.

After much thought and discussion, Dr. Geoffrey Newton, an exceptional and likeable young man, came aboard as my associate and heir-apparent in 1995. We worked extremely well together, as we were in many ways similar in temperament and work ethic. After one year, Geoff and I agreed amicably to a deal. I began to reduce my working days gradually year by year, starting in January 1997 and ultimately ending in December 2000. The practice transition was smooth and our friendship has remained strong. Occasionally we get together and play golf.

At the farewell party in December 2000, I was all choked up. Joy, peace, and gratitude infused my very being. I felt joy because my career had been productive, and was now winding down nicely, leaving me time to explore the world, and to discover the meaning of life. My mind was at peace because I knew my patients were in good hands. For my staff, I felt immense gratitude for their loyalty and good work throughout the years.

They are all individuals of integrity, compassion and they all work with love. I shall forever remember them with great fondness:

Lynne Daily served the longest on my staff as a dental hygienist. She was an excellent leader and organizer.

Henny Felato took care of business at the front office and shielded me from many demanding patients or parents.

Mary Cardile came to us as a dental assistant and later became a good dental hygienist.

Lina Trincini was my dental assistant. She kept the office running smoothly.

Juliana Jean was my one and only assistant and receptionist in my first few months of practice; later, she did the accounting and business administration. She became an indispensable help to me both in the office and at home.

Geoffrey Newton became my associate shortly after he graduated from the Orthodontic program at St. Louis University. He is an excellent orthodontist and amateur athlete.

I think the timing was perfect for me when I retired from my practice in 2000, although I continued to do some part-time teaching at university and practised one day a week at my son's office until December 2006. My very light schedule allowed me the time to develop other interests: playing golf, attending classes in creative and memoir writing, going to the library almost weekly, and reading books on many subjects, particularly philosophy and comparative religions. Lately, I often go to lectures on the immigration and activities of the Chinese in Canada, and the history of the Japanese invasions of China, Korea, and South Asia. I do my exercises and tai chi daily and feel fine. Retirement has been good to me. Once in a while, I reflect on my career and its modest accomplishments:

When I completed my program in 1968, I was welcomed to the teaching staff of the Department of Orthodontics. I believe I was the first Chinese-Canadian orthodontist in Ontario; I helped to found the Chinese Canadian Dental Society of Ontario in 1971, and was elected its first president. In 1993, I was awarded a fellowship in the International College of Dentists, a global honorary society for outstanding achievement in dentistry and service to the community.

I have been very happy with my career; Canada and my profession have been very good to me. To pay something back to my community, I volunteered to help mentoring new immigrants, to help children to read and write at a public library; I treated for free some inner-city children and I set up the Alan K. Joe and Family Scholarships at the Faculty of Dentistry. I also donated funds to help needy dental students. I like to think that I have influenced many young people to enter my profession, judging by the dozens of interviews I gave students over the years, and the numerous letters of reference that I have written for admission to different universities. I am proud of my children. Mark graduated from Tuft's Dental School in Boston, and Petina earned her degree from Boston College. My work was a good complement to my character and personality. I give credit to my mother for insisting that I go to university, to have avoided a man's worst fear. Along the way, I was very fortunate to have good mentors and inspiring teachers. I enjoyed my work and that was a true blessing for any person.

In my study, I have several photo albums of former patients who graciously allowed me to take their pictures upon completion of their treatment. A large framed photo of my former staff hangs on a wall leading to my study. Occasionally, I look at these photos and remember them all with affection. I like to think that I have fashioned my patients' smiles with a breath of my own spirit. It is this memory of my life's work, the seeds planted with tenderness and the harvest reaped with joy that I will forever cherish.

30

STELLAN AND OLIVIA

My greatest blessings call me Gung Gung, (grandfather) When their little fingers clutch my hands, my heart is forever theirs. Stellan and Olivia: the little boy belongs to Petina and her partner, Christian Kirk-Jensen; the little girl to Mark and his wife, Sonia.

Stellan was born on December 11, 2007, in France. My wife and I arrived at Petina's home in Paris on December 16. Christian, the proud father, drove Juliana Jean to the hospital, while I took a nap. Nearly three hours later, I heard the front door opening. I ran to greet mother and baby with big hugs. I held Stellan's tender little body ever so carefully, and looked into his tiny, startled eyes. My orthodontic instincts made me inspect his mouth to be sure he did not have a cleft lip or palate.

Before we left Toronto for Paris, we had seen pictures of the baby on the Internet, thanks to modern technology. In person, he looked much better, more mature, than any five-day-old infant I had ever seen. He was not only cute, he was just about perfect, with good facial balance and symmetry. His ears were shaped beautifully, and, according to Chinese folklore, that signifies long life and prosperity. Of course, I was biased.

Stellan had a ravenous appetite, and grew chubby and looked better every day. I babysat him whenever possible, giving his mother an hour or two for much needed sleep and my wife the opportunity to go shopping for groceries. I sang lullabies to him and rocked him gently to sleep. He was a very good baby. Many nights I did not hear any crying at all. One morning, when I said hello to him, he appeared to look me in the eye and smiled. I touched his hand and he clasped my fingers. He kicked his legs in the air and gurgled.

I have urged Petina and Christian to be sure that Stellan learns some Chinese. He will be dealing with the Chinese in the future, and may even work in China someday, for the same reason that my parents and I emigrated to the West in the twentieth century: to seek a better life. Therefore, I have chosen a Chinese name for Stellan – Kwok Sing Lun in Cantonese, meaning circling star. Stellan Joe Kirk-Jensen became his full name in English. My wife and I felt honoured that Petina and Christian chose my family name as their son's middle name. We have set up a scholarship fund for him, so that when the time comes he will be able to attend university anywhere in the world. Of course, we hope he will do so in Canada.

In 2006, a highlight for us was the beautiful wedding of our son, Mark, and his beloved Sonia Choi in Maui, Hawaii. The big day arrived sunny and warm on Thursday, November 9. We woke up by seven "o'clock" to bright sunshine, and we all gathered at dockside of the cruise ship *The Pride of Hawaii*, for a van to pick us up for the ride to The Wailea Golf

Club of Maui, where the ceremony was to take place.

At the Wailea, it was warm and pleasant, with a trade wind blowing gently. Two dozen white chairs were neatly arranged on the lawn of the clubhouse. A young woman holding a violin saw us walking towards the chairs, and she began to play. The air was filled with lovely music and the fragrance of flowering trees.

The ceremony was conducted by a large, jovial, native-Hawaiian clergyman, whose voice had a rich resonance that echoed across the lawns and gardens. Mark and his best man, his cousin Ian, were waiting in place. The procession started with Madeline Chang, the flower girl, and Ethan Anderson, the ring bearer, followed by Annie Anderson, Sonia's sister and the matron-of-honour. Then, the beautiful and beaming bride walked down the aisle on the arm of her proud father, Mr. Yoon-Sup Choi. Seated in the front rows were the bride's mother, Helen, my wife and I, Sonia's brother Abe, and Annie's husband, Cameron Anderson.

The invited guests who graciously came all the way from Canada were my brother and sister-in-law, Howard and Barbara (Hazel had passed away many years before), Mark's godmother, Juliana Jay, and my wife's cousin Helen Chang. Our daughter, Petina, and her companion, Christian Kirk-Jensen, joined us from Paris. The lovely surroundings created an atmosphere of simple elegance and beauty.

Six years later, the happiness of this event came back to us with the arrival of Mark and Sonia's daughter, Olivia, our granddaughter; she multiplied the joy in the lives of Juliana Jean and me. Her birth meant so much to all of us, particularly because she came late in our lives.

Christmas 2012 was extra special for all of us, because Olivia was born on December 14, five days before her father's birthday, three days after her cousin, Stellan's – and a hundred years after her great-grandfather first came to Canada. What a joyous December! Mark and Sonia named her Olivia

Ryan Joe, and my wife and I gave her a Chinese name – Lai Wah, which means "a beautiful Chinese girl."

On a warm summer day when Olivia was three, I watched her playing with her cousin Jaida on a carpet of soft green grass; she was laughing and shrieking for joy, while cartwheeling and somersaulting. Such exuberance! At the breakfast table on many mornings, I look at her photos on the wall. I see a happy chubby face with a little flat nose smiling back at me. A white headband with a white carnation adorns her shiny hair; her eyes sparkle, while two tiny bottom teeth peek through her open mouth. Olivia and Stellan are truly a divine blessing, perhaps compensating us for growing old. We are blessed to have a little boy and a little girl to adore.

31

ZEST FOR LIFE – A NEW GAME

Golf was an intriguing new game that Juliana Jean and I took up very late in life. Previously, I liked tennis and ballroom dancing the most. However, when I was in my early sixties, back and leg problems prevented me from playing tennis anymore. Fortunately, some months later, my wife and I discovered golf.

Our present home backs onto the Saint George's Golf and Country Club, with our sundeck facing the sixteenth tee, some thirty-five yards away. Yet, for some twenty years the idea of hitting and chasing a little white ball all over the place, tapping it into a three-inch hole, was not our idea of fun. Then, around 1998, our friends Fred and Louise Mark invited us out to play golf with them. Previously, Juliana Jean and I had taken a few lessons on the driving range, but were nervous to go onto an actual course to play by ourselves. Golfing rules and etiquette sounded confusing to us.

For our first game ever, the Marks took us to a short executive course called Cresthaven. It was much shorter and easier to play than a regular course, which is usually more than two or three times longer, and contains a lot more hazards, such as ponds, woods, and hundreds of other places where you can lose your balls.

When I stepped onto that rounded patch of grass called the first tee, I tried to place the brand-new ball on a thin wooden stick, but the ball kept falling off as my fingers wobbled. Two youths and their fathers were standing a few yards away, waiting for their turn to tee off; I was sure their eyes were trained on me. As I stood over my ball and got ready to hit, I mentally went over all the steps that I should remember: the grip, alignment, stance, ball position, weight shift, as well as some basic advice from the Marks about keeping the head still and not looking up too soon. These thoughts filled my mind.

Seconds later, I swung. My ball sliced weakly to the right and dribbled more to the side than forward. I sheepishly walked to my ball and hit my next shot, which flew high and looked nice, but shot way over the flag; I had to chip it back onto the green on my third shot. I then three-putted for a treble bogey, six strokes! My friends had each made par, while my wife had hit her first shot straight down the fairway and bounced it onto the green. She two-putted the ball into the hole and laughed happily. I wanted to dig a big hole and crawl into it!

Golf is a strange game. It calls for skill, character, strategy, and luck. Its unique fascination is based on the fact that, while you may play against the golf course, a competitor, and the day's elements, your chief opponent is yourself. You alone determine how you play; it is as much a mental game as a physical one. I have found that the harder you try, the worse you get. A relaxed mind and body seemed to provide the best chance for a good and enjoyable game.

Golf in many ways mirrors life, as it embraces pleasure and despair. Very rarely does the ball go exactly where you want it to go, but you need to accept this graciously. I have seen golfers throwing their clubs into a lake after some bad shots. Once, on television, I saw John Daly, a famous American golfer who had won many major tournaments, do exactly that! However, all will come back to play again, when the day is sunny, the breeze is caressing, and you need an excuse from work or household chores. In your mind's eye, you may hit a long ball perfectly on the club's sweet spot, hear the melodious ping sound, and see the ball soar straight and true towards the flag. The feeling is "Wow!" For a second or two, you may feel it is you who is flying over the trees and the fairway to glide down to a patch of green, like an angel with wings. Golf can even be a spiritual experience.

Golf can also provide an opportunity for the expression of noble qualities, such as honesty, courtesy, and generosity. It is a test of honour and sportsmanship, because one can cheat by kicking the ball a few inches onto a better spot when nobody is looking or by claiming you have found your "lost ball" when you did not. You can also make subtle movements to distract your opponent. One can be a gentleman or a jerk on the course.

While a golfer's battle against self is a strong appeal of the game, there are many other attractions that will bring the golfer to the course again and again. The great outdoors is always alluring, particularly to us city folks. The rolling hills, valleys, lakes, and rivers that are found on nearly all courses are always pleasing to the eye. At our course, Islington Golf Club, the vegetation and fauna change dramatically with the seasons. The lush velvety green of spring changes to the bright orange and red of autumn; Mimico Creek, which meanders through the fairways of our club, may present a torrent of icy water in April and a slow trickle in August, and provide frequent sightings of wild ducks and geese frolicking in the river or marching on our fairways.

My wife and I love golf and the companionship of the folks who play the game the right way, with sportsmanship and courtesy. Golf has given us a zest in life and we enjoy playing together much of the time. This new game has brought us closer, and we have made many new friends. At the end of a day, it is marvellous to sit with friends in the lounge or on the outdoor patio, telling tales and watching the setting sun bathe the lush greens, as we sip a refreshing lemonade or beer. At such moments, I feel very grateful to the Almighty for His wondrous gift to us, this enchanting game called golf.

32

TAI CHI – MEDITATION IN MOTION

Tai chi and meditation, when complemented by a proper balance of work, play, and spirituality, have given me health and happiness. Early in my career, I realized that practising dentistry was stressful, particularly after I read that, according to insurance statistics, dentists have an alarming suicide rate, the highest among all the professionals. I was worried by that knowledge. At that time, I was working with many physically and/or mentally challenged children at the Hospital for Sick Children, and with socially handicapped ones at the Children's Aid Society. In order to cope with the extra demands, I turned to smoking, about six to seven cigarettes each day. I realized that I had to learn to relax and develop a strategy that could help me to enjoy my work more, and have a long career.

Tai chi is a discipline that promotes physical, mental, and spiritual health. It had its beginning in ancient China as a martial art, but like most people all over the world these days, I do it as a gentle and meditative exercise for relaxation, fitness, and spirituality. Tai chi means "supreme ultimate," the concept that all of life is comprised of the perpetual interplay of two vital energies, Yin and Yang. Tai chi can be practised by persons of all ages, strong or weak, and anywhere with a few feet of space, most often gardens and parks. Some people call it a slow form of shadow boxing. The ballet-like movements require proper deep breathing, relaxed posture, weight shifting, inner calmness, and correct technique. It can relieve high blood pressure, muscle and joint pain, and other physical and mental problems. Respected institutions, such as the Mayo Clinic and Harvard Medical School, have reported that tai chi is one of the best exercises for good health.

My interest in tai chi started many years ago when I noticed that my mother and her friends were practising it daily, and they looked to me calm and healthy. They could also bend to touch their toes from a standing position. My family physician and good friend Dr. Margaret Tao was also interested in learning tai chi, and, on her recommendation, my wife and I joined her in taking lessons with Madame Chan, an expert in the Yang style of tai chi, one of several popular styles practised in China. We took weekly lessons at Madame Chan's home for eight months. I learned some one hundred and eight moves, which took nearly half an hour to work through. These days, I am a little lazy, and thus each morning I do about eight minutes of calisthenics, and then do the shorter forms of tai chi for ten minutes. A total of about eighteen minutes is good enough for me, before my stomach growls for breakfast.

I also have incorporated deep breathing, called chi-kung, or qigong, into my tai chi movements. Chi-kung brings more fresh oxygen to the body, and exhales more impurities from the lungs. I believe these measures have enhanced my immune system, my health, and my spirituality.

After learning tai chi and chi-kung, I felt calmer, less tense, enjoyed my work more, and stopped smoking totally. This mindset has stayed with me for over forty years, and now into my retirement. These days I play golf about three or four times a week. Before each game I usually do a few minutes of tai chi exercises as a warm-up, then walk the nine or eighteen holes while playing. Each game takes about four hours and fifteen minutes.

As I get older, I realize more clearly the necessity of maintaining physical and mental health. I am studying tai chi in more depth, particularly its spiritual dimensions. Tai chi teaches that the universe is circular and perpetually in motion, with night, Yin, following day, Yang. A human being is like a tiny universe, more marvellously designed than any machine, but it needs harmonious movement and rhythm. The laws of nature should be observed, with naturalness, roundness, and softness in all our motions. The symbol of tai chi is a circle divided into two parts of equal size, one being Yin/black and the other Yang/white. The two elements are equal and are complementary, interacting with each other. This symbol also shows a touch of black within white and white within black: nothing is absolute and everything in this universe is relative and interconnected. Balance of the body and mind enriches our spirit and our zest for life.

Tai chi and meditation have become a way of life for me. I have learned to meditate while doing my tai chi movements. It calms the mind as it reduces the chatter and static of daily living. These mental and physical exercises have opened up my senses to people and nature. I have gained patience and equanimity, and I am less likely to get caught up with negative reactions, worries, and despair, and more likely to be at peace with myself.

33

WORK, PLAY, LOVE, AND SPIRITUALITY

In addition to tai chi, the four words: Work, Play, Love, and Spirituality have guided my daily living. I am trying to give attention to each of these every day.

The pursuit of a spiritual life is an aspiration common to all of us. I have found my spiritual journey exceedingly difficult and confusing, because I have been greatly influenced by Buddhism, Confucianism, and Christianity, and slightly touched by Taoism, which I understand the least. Taoism, which is also known as Daoism, is a mystical philosophical tradition of the Chinese, which was based on the writings of Lao-tsu from some 2,600 years ago. It emphasizes living in harmony with nature and the Tao; it has cosmological notions of Yin-Yang, Feng-Shui, and Shamanic elements.

Very early in my childhood, my mother regularly took me to Buddhist temples. We prayed, bowed, and burned incense in front of a smiling goddess sitting on a cushion of lotus flowers. We called her Quan Yin, or Kuan Yan in other dialects. She is also known as the Goddess of Compassion and Mercy, a cosmic being, like an angel or saint in Christianity. I think of her as a manifestation of the Divine Mother Mary. I have seen paintings and sculptures of Quan Yin holding an infant, similar to the Madonna and Child.

My mother lost her first-born son when he was a child, and after many years of fervent prayers, I was born, so Mother was extremely grateful to Quan Yin. She always took me with her to pay my respects to this loving goddess, who was dressed in flowing white robes, smiling at me. Mother told me Quan Yin was my spiritual godmother, who would answer my calls whenever I needed her.

K'ung Fu-tzu, known as Confucius in the West, has been the dominant moral force in China for the past twenty-six centuries. This supreme Chinese sage had influence over every aspect of life in China, until Mao Zedong and the Communists tried to do away with ancient customs and beliefs. At an early age, I heard about Confucius, mostly from Master Hung, a college professor of ethnic Hakka heritage, who lived downstairs from us. I was a curious adolescent and enjoyed talking to him. He explained about the teachings of Confucius: filial piety, integrity, thrift, and respect for tradition, elders, and ancestors. He also told me about other famous men in Chinese history, such as Lao-tsu, who was said to be the founder of Taoism and the Cosmology of Yin and Yang. I could not understand much of it at the time, but my interest was aroused.

My first contact with Christianity came from a close family friend, Grandma Lin Tong, who was a devout Baptist. Most Sundays, she would try to get Mother and me to go to church with her and her family. Often, we did go with her. The old lady could not read or write, but she could tell us wonderful stories about Jesus and His miracles. I truly loved Grandma Lin Tong, who lived to be nearly a hundred years old. She had bound feet, and walked with a wobbling gait, but she still managed to walk up three flights of stairs to visit my mother and me. In her home, I was intrigued by a picture of a strange-looking man with long, brownish hair, a beard, and blue eyes. She told me that he was Yeh-so in Cantonese, the Son of God who had come to earth to save us.

My experience of Christianity was strengthened in 1946, when Grandma Lin Tong convinced Mother to send me for Grade 1 to Pui Ching Elementary School, which was founded by American Baptists. We heard many Bible stories; I was taught that Jesus was the perfect revelation of God in man, the only Son of God. I learned to sing in Cantonese, "Jesus loves me, this I know / For the Bible tells me so." It was a loving, attractive message.

Each year our school held a three-day evangelical rally. On the last day, we were called to convert. Many of my classmates answered the call to come to Christ. I was nearly ready, but I had a few reservations. If I converted, I would have to give up going with my Mother to pay respect to the goddess Quan Yin, who had helped Mother and me so much in the past, particularly during the war. I was also told by a Christian neighbour that we would need to remove from our house the altars that venerated our ancestors. She said only statues or pictures of Jesus should be shown: anything else was idolatry. It sounded like I would have to relinquish my old habits and cultural past. I was unsettled, and realized that I was not ready to commit myself.

After arriving in Toronto in 1950, I regularly attended the United Church of Canada on Chestnut Street. My stepmother Dai Ma took me there regularly every Sunday. The Reverend David Lee was friendly and kind to me, but his sermons were rather dull. After five years, I left that church without converting.

In 1962, I travelled through Europe and the Middle East. I was very keen to visit Jerusalem and to seek Jesus. In July, I found myself in Jerusalem, and was very impressed with the sights and sounds of this historical city. I

visited the Al-Aqsa Mosque, the church of the Holy Sepulchre, the Western
Wailing Wall, and other historical places. I walked the Via Dolorosa, the
road on which Jesus carried the cross to Calvary.

On my last day in Jerusalem, from an upper floor of our hotel, I surveyed
the magnificent skyline of this Holy City, bathed in the glorious evening
sun. Majestic buildings of worship shone in gold, Christian or Muslim or
Jewish. I could not help but ask myself, "Is the Truth one of these, none
of these, or all of these?" Jerusalem was a divided city, with much hostility
among the different religious groups. Even among the various Christian
churches, there was discernible disharmony.

I knelt by the window of my room and prayed for inspiration. Unfortunately, none came to me. I left Jerusalem disappointed, without any
answers. I was more confused.

After returning to Canada, I rarely attended a church service until
around the time of my marriage to Juliana Jean. First, I took some lessons
in Roman Catholicism at Saint Basil's, and later went fairly regularly with
my wife and children to different Catholic churches in Toronto. I enjoyed
singing the hymns, but did not like the sermons much, which were mostly
uninspiring.

Judaism, Christianity, and Islam share a belief in one God and teach
peace, love of God, and compassion to mankind. Yet they seem unable to
stop their deadly wars with each other, sometimes indulging in killing for
the sake of narrow religious orthodoxy. To seek more knowledge, I have
taken several extension courses at the University of Toronto on philosophy
and world religions.

After much thought and earnest searching, this is my current thinking
regarding the traditions dear to my heart. I believe that Confucianism
has been valuable for the Chinese, their history and culture, but is mostly
outdated in this day and age. Much of Confucius's teaching is too rigid,
feudal, static, and perhaps a hindrance to China's progress in the modern

world. However, I still value his teaching on morality and filial piety. I think it is a philosophy which is still relevant to some degree, but it is not really a religion, because God is not part of its belief.

Christianity is inspiring, and I have been impressed with the Christian tradition of service to God and humanity. Christians have done enormous good in caring for the sick, the poor, and the downtrodden. Many missionaries and their families have suffered and sacrificed so much in trying to save souls for Jesus, some dying in foreign lands from tropical diseases and political upheavals.

These days, I am heartened to see that more Jews, Christians, Muslims, Buddhists, and others have initiated dialogue and reconciliation. Pope Francis appeared to be enlightened, doing much good work for world peace and harmony. I think he respects other traditions and believes in spiritual connectivity. I hope that we can all live in peaceful co-existence, without claiming supremacy for one particular Faith, and the need to propagate that belief to all people. Unfortunately, that day still seems to be far away.

I had, on a couple occasions, wondered if God is a delusion, created by mankind's desire for a Supreme Being, who created for us the marvellous wonders of the universe, a validation of human life, and help in times of need. Humans may pray for rain, for victory in battle, for eternal life, and so much more. But many believers accept religious dogma purely on faith. They embrace their faith wholeheartedly, as taught by their family or clergy, without much critical thought. I sometimes envy those people, wishing I could readily accept beliefs with less questioning and skepticism.

In the past few years, I have become very interested in Buddhism, the faith of my mother. What the Gautama Buddha taught in India some 2,600 years ago was a philosophy of understanding the meaning of existence, learning ways to live skilfully with love and compassion, and minimizing suffering. He did not set out to found a religion or claim any divine wisdom. The Buddha stated that he was an enlightened human being, not a God or prophet of a God. He discouraged talks of the existence of God. Many years and centuries later, when Buddhism arrived in places like Tibet, China, Vietnam, and Japan, it took on indigenous traditions. Local people added cultural details to Buddhism, giving it different looks and stereotypes. In China, The Buddha has been elevated to godly status, with statues and temples built in his honour for worship, which was not what The Lord Buddha had intended.

The revered Quan Yin is a Chinese version of a Buddhist bodhisattva, like a saint in Christianity. My mother – and I in my youth – believed Quan Yin was a true goddess. Some people think that Buddhism has too many idols and superstitions, but I think this became common to all religions, in varying degrees, as they evolved over the centuries. Of the major religions that I have studied, I have found Buddhism to be more inclusive and tolerant towards other beliefs. One of the teachings is that life is impermanent, like a breath; it ends when the breathing stops, but is followed by birth. Existence is cyclical, with neither a beginning nor an end. We must cherish the present moment. Buddhism is more oriented to philosophy and less to a belief in a Supreme Being. I think Faith is an essential concept of Christianity, with total devotion to an almighty Creator.

Is our world big enough for so many religions to coexist peacefully? I certainly hope so. Whatever name we use to call our Creator – God, Lord, or Allah – is not important, as long as we are loving and compassionate, because a Supreme Being would not be so petty as to care what we humans may call Him. The Divine is far beyond our understanding.

My Chinese and North American upbringings have challenged me to look more deeply into faith and spirituality; I think all religious systems possess a piece of the Universal Truth, but not necessarily the only Truth. For me, I want to be happy and make others happy, to let my heart touch my head in dealing with other people. I like to be faithful and truthful, and to live life as simply as possible, with loving kindness and an appreciation for nature and all sentient beings. At the end of my journey on earth, I hope to leave no unpaid debts, unhealthy thoughts, and no regrets. This is my spiritual journey, my quest.

34

REDEMPTION FOR
A VILLAGE

Should I revisit a place that I had hated? When I got older, I felt it was my duty to return for a visit to honour my ancestors, even though my years of living there, under Japanese occupation, was nightmarish. In fact, when my mother was alive, every few years I had asked her if she would like to revisit our ancestral village, Nam Bin. Each time she had shaken her head and muttered, "No. I have seen the village already too often, in my dreams, horrible ones," and I could detect a tightening of her jaw muscles. However, in more recent years, I felt a desire to find closure for the uneasy relationship I had with Nam Bin. So, in 2013, I decided to accompany Pak Sing, a cousin's son, to visit the old village.

On the morning of November 25, Juliana Jean and I set out from the home of Susan and Ed Kong, who lived in the country town of Foo Shan, about a hundred miles from Hong Kong. We were their guests for the week, and they were kind enough to lend us their car and chauffeur for the day's journey. Our driver, Mr. Fung, drove us for about two hours on a new highway to the town of Xin Hui Sang. As previously arranged, in a hotel lobby, we were to meet Pak Sing from Hong Kong and the tenant of our house in Nam Bin, Mr. Chow Buck Dick. He was a retired farmer, and had been living with his wife in our home for over forty years. Dung Sew was Buck Dick's mother, and she had occasionally been my babysitter during the war. When we left the village in 1945, my mother let Dung Sew move into our place, and her family had stayed there ever since.

After we had a simple-but-tasty lunch at the hotel, with freshly caught shrimps and fish from nearby rivers, free-range chicken, and Chinese bok choi greens, we drove about half an hour on a paved country road to reach the village. I recognized the old watchtower instantly, as I had climbed it a few times.

Buck Dick led the way and, within two or three minutes of walking, we were met at the front of the old house by his wife, son, and daughter. One of my first questions was about my old babysitter, and I was informed that Dung Sew had passed away, at the age of ninety-four. I had missed meeting her by three months. I felt regret, as she was the only person in the whole village that I could remember with any fondness.

From the outside, our house still looked in decent shape. It had been built with grey bricks in the 1890s, by my grandfather, Yuk Goh, for his four sons. At the time and for nearly a hundred years, villagers had called it The Big House, because it was the largest and best house among the mostly humble dwellings of poor farmers. Because the four apartments faced a central courtyard, with an open skylight, the bedrooms were dark. Each room had only one naked light bulb hung from the ceiling. Buck Dick used a flashlight to show us where the wooden support beams had begun to rot. I promised to discuss preserving this heritage house with the rest of the Joe family.

On a shallow wooden ledge at the back of the parlour were photos of my grandfather and grandmother, printed on ceramic plaques. I walked closer and solemnly bowed three times to them. Buck Dick's wife told me that she regularly placed incense and fruit in front of my grandparents, to show respect and seek permission to live peacefully in the house. Country folks are superstitious and afraid of spirits and ghosts.

After half an hour of looking around, I asked Buck Dick to take me to see the Monument of Martyrs of the Revolution. Within three minutes of driving up the county road, we arrived at a large clearing surrounded by bamboo and flowers. The granite monument stood majestically, about eighteen feet high. I looked closely and found Lai Ho's name. I stood silent, trying hard to remember how he had read me stories and played with me. My hand reached forward and brushed away some dirt from his name. I solemnly bowed to him three times and quietly walked away.

We returned to the house to say goodbye to the Chow family. They invited us to stay for dinner, but we had to get back to Foo Shan on time. Buck Dick's wife gave each of us a bagful of local fruit and a valued local product called *chun pei*, a sun-dried tangerine skin, preserved in a special way. It smells fragrant and tastes sweet. Cantonese use it as a condiment; my wife likes to put some little pieces of it in soups and rice congees.

As we walked away from the village, I looked up at the old watchtower. I was tempted to go in and climb to the top, but Buck Dick warned me that the steps were unsafe.

Upon leaving, I felt comfortable with the good folks living in our old house and, with the renovations and continued maintenance, it might still be there for future generations. I realized that history and circumstances are beyond the control of us humans and departed ancestors. Our sufferings were not the fault of the village. The landscape was probably the same as in my father's time, with fish ponds, lush green bamboo, and verdant rice paddies nearby. Now, however, it was modernized, with paved roads, private automobiles, and TV antennas. Glancing back at the hands waving farewell from the shade of a banyan tree and the watchtower, I wondered if I or my spirit would ever return to this land of my forefathers. I doubted it, for I had travelled far and wide to the Four Seas. With the ghosts of those village years expurgated, I felt redeemed and at peace.

35

RECONCILIATION
AT MOUNT PLEASANT

The Chinese are known to worship ancestors, but I think it might be more correct to say that we like to remember and honour our ancestors, particularly at their gravesites. This is our way to express homage, and is not about our religious beliefs. Visiting the cemetery, called *qing ming*, or "tomb sweeping," normally takes place in the third lunar month, around April 4 or 5 in the Gregorian calendar.

Each spring around the time of Qing Ming, a festival for tomb sweeping, I would go with my mother and other relatives to the graves of my grandparents. In front of their tombstone we offered roasted pork, tea, and wine, and burnt joss sticks and play money. This was done in the hope that our grandpa and grandma would not lack food or money in their afterlife. We bowed, and then lit firecrackers to drive away evil spirits. Nothing was wasted, as we would then have a picnic or take the food home.

In Canada, each spring I would take my Christian family to Mount Pleasant Cemetery to pay respects to my father, Dai Ma, and my mother. We would bring flowers for planting, usually hardy geraniums. We prayed for blessings and bowed to each three times.

In the summer of 2012, my daughter and her four-year-old son flew in from Paris, France, to Toronto. One day, Petina wanted to visit the graves of my parents; particularly dear to her was my mother, her Por Por, who babysat her and bought her sweets. Stellan came along with us, as we felt that he was old enough to learn about life and death.

We drove to Section 52 of Mount Pleasant Cemetery, where my father and Dai Ma were buried. I dug two holes, while Petina planted two pots of geraniums. Stellan helped to water them. He followed our lead and bowed three times to my father and Dai Ma. After we tidied the gravesite, we walked approximately seventy yards to my mother's grave in Section 49. I explained to him that my mother, his mommy's beloved Por Por, was buried under the large patch of grass and the lovely jade-green tombstone. On it was inscribed in big letters the name JOE; below, on the right side, was my mother's name in English, and also her Chinese name in a vertical line. I told Stellan that someday in the future his grandma and I will be buried on the left side of the plot.

Then I asked him, "Stellan, someday I'll be buried underneath here. Will you come to visit me sometime, and bow to me like you just did to your Mommy's grandma?"

"Oh yes, Gung Gung, I will. But I don't want you to die! Gung Gung, you are my friend. I love you. Don't die. I love you!"

He looked up at me, his eyes brimming with tears. I picked him up and, as my face touched his, I whispered, "Don't cry, Stellan. Gung Gung is going to live for a long time. I still have to teach you how to play golf and take you to China to climb the Great Wall and see the beautiful palaces in Beijing."

He smiled through his tears. A profound emotion surged in me and I thought, "How precious it is to be loved by a child, who says to your face, I love you."

Petina and I finished planting the geraniums, added topsoil, pulled out weeds, and poured water over the stone to wash away the dirt and bird droppings. Stellan used his little pail to water the plants. All three of us bowed to my mother three times. Before we left, Petina asked for a little more time, so that she could be alone with her Por Por for a few minutes.

With Stellan holding my hand and skipping along, we walked back to my father's grave. Standing before my father, I thought of him and reminisced.

My father had worked hard all his life and helped so many relatives. He did arrange for my coming to Canada, so that I had opportunities for education and a good life and at the same time avoided the brutal years of living under communism. What my mother and I went through was not uncommon for many Chinese families, considering the culture and circumstances of the era.

Perhaps now he was aware that the world and China had changed so much in recent decades, and that his children and grandchildren have made themselves at home, establishing themselves successfully in the mainstream of the beautiful land called Gold Mountain.

I remembered what Howard said to me at one of his birthday parties: that he and I were fortunate to have lived long lives, while our father was not so lucky. For many of his sixty-two years he suffered with hepatitis and borderline diabetes. My brother added, "The stress and worries over the fate of your mother and you during the war also took a toll on him. BaBa was never very expressive or demonstrative, so he might not have said much to you, but he loved all of us."

Standing in the sunshine and taking several deep breaths of the crisp, morning air, I felt closer to my father than ever before.

Looking at his Chinese name engraved on the headstone, I conjured up the image of my father introducing me proudly to his friends on my first Sunday in Toronto, when he took me to Chinatown. I bowed to him three more times, and, with no more hesitation, I whispered to him the words I wished I had said so many years ago. "BaBa, I love you."

36

REFLECTIONS

These are my heartfelt stories. I consider myself a lucky man, with so many blessings. My past has been memorable, full of engaging stories; my present is good, as I have health, a loving family, and sufficient savings to retire. I enjoy golfing and writing stories. The future looks golden as I pursue my lifelong interests in history, philosophy, and literature. However, I'm most eager to be doing grandfatherly activities, like playing with my grandchildren in a park, reciting little poems, or singing children's songs.

To my family, friends, and readers, I hope that you are pleased to know me better. For my children and grandchildren, I hope that you are happy to have known me. I am proud of you, for you have integrated some of the best values of the East and West; all of you have the unique opportunities to contribute to a new world order. I believe that the future of the world should not be dominated by one race, one nation, or one religion. It should be a world society in which all human beings can live in peace on this earth while reaching outward to the stars. This is only a dream at this time of global violence, but I do hope it will happen, eventually.

The ox and the unicorn have captured my imagination; they are my guiding spirits. In the Chinese zodiac, the ox is better known as the water buffalo; it is a hardworking and respected animal, indispensable to farmers throughout Chinese history. The unicorn, on the other hand, is a noble, spiritual creature in mythology. I am happy to have been born an ox, to have laboured and achieved modest success in life. However, I am most proud to have attained a little of the qualities attributed to the unicorn, to have lived a life aptly described by Ralph Waldo Emerson, American philosopher:

> To laugh often and much; to win the respect of intelligent people and the affection of children; to earn the appreciation of honest critics and endure the betrayal of false friends; to appreciate beauty, to find the best in others; to leave the world a little better, whether by a healthy child, a garden, or a redeemed social condition; to know even one life has breathed easier because you have lived. This is to have succeeded.

Some time ago, my daughter was reading a draft of my memoir, and asked me how would I wish to be remembered someday. I thought about it for a few days to come up with what I thought might be suitable for my epitaph:

> He was born a stubborn Ox,
> With the blessing of the Unicorn.
> Not ever devious like a fox,
> Nor does he lie or scorn.
> He was never too wild,
> But indelible was his smile.

Mark's wedding to Sonia Choi in Hawaii, November 9, 2006

Petina, with my grandson, Stellan, 2008

My granddaughter, Olivia, 2012

Juliana Jean and I (left) with my former staff, the wonderful
team at the clinic at the Islington Golf Club, 2002
From left: me, Juliana Jean, Henny Felato, Mary Cardile,
Dr. Geoff Newton, Lynne Dailey, Lina Tricinci

The 40th anniversary of my orthodontics class, 2008
Front row, left to right: me, Ray Bozek, Eric Luks
Back row, left to right: Roland (Rolly) Albert, Bryan Smith, Bill
Sinclair, Gavin James (Gavin joined our class in our second year.)

Return to Nam Bin, in an area called Tienjin
Juliana Jean and I in front of the entrance gate

The old watchtower,
Juliana Jean and I standing
with Chow Che King, my
cousin from Hong Kong

Juliana Jean and I with our tenants, Chow Buck Dick and his family (and dog), in front of my ancestral home in 2013

My 80th birthday celebration on the Danish island of Bornholm, July 21, 2017, celebrating with (left to right) Christian, Juliana Jean, Petina and Stellan, Sonia, and Mark, with Olivia

Stellan and Olivia playing checkers in a market square in Bornholm

NOTE

1. Best-selling author James Bradley, in his book *The China Mirage* (Little, Brown and Company, 2015), exposes the hidden truths behind the trade of opium into China by both British and Americans in the 1800s. He described how these traders corrupted the Chinese; my grandfather's downfall was partly attributable to opium.

   I learned that Britain made huge fortunes from the opium trade, in part to buy Chinese tea. The British were breaking their own law as well as Chinese law, by smuggling opium cultivated in India. This illegal activity triggered the Opium War, in which the Chinese were defeated by the superior arms and technology of the British, and were forced to pay huge indemnities and cede the island of Hong Kong to Britain. In addition, four other ports had to open for the entry of this drug and other goods. Some American merchants also cashed in on this business by transporting this narcotic from Turkey to sell in China. President Franklin Delano Roosevelt's maternal grandfather, Warren Delano, was known to have made a fortune in this business when he worked in Hong Kong on two occasions.

BIBLIOGRAPHY

Abrams, Douglas, His Holiness the Dalai Lama, and Archbishop Desmond Tutu. *The Book of Joy: Lasting Happiness in a Changing World*. New York: Avery / Penguin Random House LLC, 2016.

Bernstein, Richard. *Ultimate Journey: Retracing the Path of an Ancient Buddhist Monk Who Crossed Asia in Search of Enlightenment*. New York: Alfred A. Knopf, 2001.

Bradley, James. *The China Mirage: The Hidden History of American Disaster in Asia*. New York: Little Brown and Company, 2015.

Bradley, James. *Flyboys: A True Story of Courage*. New York: Little, Brown and Company, 2003.

Bradley, James. *The Imperial Cruise: A Secret History of Empire and War*. Boston: Back Bay Books / Little, Brown and Company, 2009.

Chan, Arlene. *The Chinese in Toronto from 1878: From Outside to Inside the Circle*. Toronto: Dundurn Press, 2011.

Chang, Iris. *The Rape of Nanjing: The Forgotten Holocaust of World War II*. New York: Basic Books, 1997.

Chu, Irene. *Rare Breed: A Chinese Jewish Quest*. Markham, Ontario: Irene C. Chu, 2016.

Gibran, Kahlil. *The Prophet*. New York: Alfred A. Knopf, 1971.

Joe, Howard. *On My Honour: An Autobiography of Howard Joe*. St. Catharines, Ontario: The Zhou Press, 2010.

Joe, Howard. *Golden Opportunities: The Contribution and Development of the Chinese in Early North America*. St. Catharines, Ontario: The Zhou Press

Li, Peter, ed. *The Search for Justice: Japanese War Crimes*. New Brunswick, New Jersey: Transaction Publishers, 2008.

Matsuoka, Tamaki. *Torn Memories of Nanjing: Testimonies of Japanese War Veterans and Chinese Survivors of the Nanjing Massacres*. Toronto: ALPHA Education, 2016.

Morris, Seymour, Jr. *Supreme Commander: MacArthur's Triumph in Japan*. New York: Harper Collins Publishing, 2014.

Poy, Vivienne. *A River Named Lee*. Scarborough, Ontario: Calyan Publishing Ltd., 1995.

ABOUT THE AUTHOR

Alan Joe was born in 1937 in the city of Canton (Guangzhou), China. That year, the Japanese invaded China, and he and his mother were forced to flee to their ancestral village.

After the war, Alan attended missionary school in Canton, but in 1949 the Communists took control of mainland China. He then fled to Canada with an uncle. Settling in Toronto in 1950, he began his schooling in Grade Two, learned English, and eventually graduated from the University of Toronto with a Doctor of Dental Surgery degree and a Certification in Orthodontics.

Alan taught at the Faculty of Dentistry, University of Toronto, and practised in West Toronto, serving as president of the Chinese Canadian Dental Society in 1971–72. In 1993, he received a Fellowship from the International College of Dentists.

After retirement, Alan took courses in memoir writing and creative writing. His other activities include ballroom dancing, Tai Chi, meditation, studying philosophy and comparative religion, reading, golfing, and travelling. He has also volunteered in Toronto at the public library, at Mt. Sinai Hospital, and with new immigrants.

Alan is married, and has two children and two grandchildren. He lives with his wife in Toronto and St. Petersburg, Florida.

He can be reached at *alanjoesstory@gmail.com* and on *Facebook*.